Just Another Brick

Mel Phillips

Just Another Brick

Published in 2009 in association with
Absolute Design Solutions.

ISBN 978-0-9552139-8-4

A CIP catalogue of this book is available from the
British Library.

Typeset by Rachel Jones
Absolute Design Solutions
www.absolutedesignsolutions.co.uk

Illustrations by Joelle Brindley
joelle@off-kuff.co.uk.

Printed and bound in the UK by
JEM Digital Print Services, Whitstable, Kent.

This book is dedicated to all those pedagogues who are still scaling that old chalk face.

"Hey! Teachers! Leave them kids alone!
...All in all you're just another brick in the
wall."

PINK FLOYD 1979

Introduction

There have been quite a lot of books written about school children and their funny little anecdotes, but I can't think of a book that has been written about teachers.

We teachers are a strange breed, because we live perpetually within the education system. Pupil, to student, and then the subsequent return to school as a member of staff.

These true stories are about some of the wacky, eccentric, and funny colleagues whom I have taught with over the years. I count myself as one of these too!

College Days

I had always wanted to be a teacher like my Auntie Sue, a games teacher. I also fancied the long holidays that came with the job!

When I had completed my A-level studies, I applied to Barry Teacher Training College in order to gain a place on their Advanced Wing course in P.E..

I had always been quite good at games. However, there was not a huge range of sporting activities open to you at Pembroke Grammar School. You either chose hockey and joined Mrs Tapleys' tough band of girls or, (as we thought) the softer option of netball with Miss Williams. You were not allowed to do both as there weren't enough games teachers. Similarly, when it came to summer sports you had to make the choice between rounders or tennis. Again we decided that only the tough girls opted for rounders whilst all the prissy, poncey girls opted for tennis. The result was that I had no knowledge of netball or tennis.

I waltzed off for my interview at Barry expecting to be accepted on the grounds that I played in the hockey and rounders teams. The interview went very badly from the outset. It materialised that the 'Dragon' in charge of the PE department had sent out letters to each prospective applicant informing them to arrive with games kit, ready for the sporting activities test. Unfortunately, I had not received one. When I informed her of this, she sighed wearily and tossed me a pair of shorts that would have fitted King Kong!

The test commenced. The hockey was no trouble to me, the same went for athletics and gym. Then came the netball demonstration. 'This is easy,' I thought, as the ball was passed to me. I ran like mad with it, only to be pulled up short.

"Have you ever played netball?" the lecturer wanted to know.

"No," I said.

"Or tennis?" she enquired, as some time later the ball fiopped into the net, time and time again.

"We will let you know by letter if you have been accepted," she said. She did. I was raving mad, and decided that if I couldn't do games I wasn't going anywhere.

"You will have to change subjects," said Mam, tactlessly. "Nobody will have you in a P.E. college if you can't play half the sports. What about Cartrefie College in Wrexham?"

I looked listlessly at their prospectus, and tossed it to one side.

"You could do R.E." Mam said.

I picked up the prospectus again and fiicked through, not even bothering to read it properly. I did notice however, that the RE course was exactly the same syllabus as I had done for A-level. 'Mightn't be so bad after all,' I thought. I had kept all the notes. If I couldn't do games, I would do R.E. and sit on my arse doing nothing for three years! The idea appealed, and I applied for a place at Cartrefie College, Wrexham.

The college turned out to be a hole, with hardly any permanent buildings. The student accommodation was comprised of a long row of Nissan huts. The tutors were literally begging students to come in. This will do, I thought, still smarting from my rejection at Barry. I accepted. On the way out of the main building I saw a lot of female students milling around.

"Where are all the boys?" I asked one girl.

"There aren't any, this is a girl's college."

That would teach me to read the prospectus properly. Crap college. A nine-hour train journey home, and a total absence of the opposite sex. Bloody great.

Actually it was great. Wonderful fun. I qualified after three years as a religious education teacher, with English and drama as my subsidiary subjects. All I had to do now was to get a job. There was no such a thing as a gap year then. All I would have got was a gap in my teeth from my father, if I hadn't already got one!

I wanted a job in Wales. I didn't want to apply anywhere else. Mid Glamorgan will suit me, I thought. I can come home every weekend from Cardiff. However, it materialised that most of the student teachers in Wales were of the same mind, so the authority had their pick. Also, those students who had attended Barry (GRRR!) or Cardiff, were, quite rightly, at the top of their list. There was no chance for me, who had dared to choose North Wales, over the capital.

I applied for many jobs, but all to no avail.

"Plenty of jobs going in the Midlands," said Mam.

"I'm not going to England."

"We didn't put you through college for you to do bugger all at the end of three years. Get some applications in now before the term starts in September."

Consequently, I found myself packed, and off to a very rough part of the Midlands, to embark on what was to be, a very long and colourful teaching career.

First School

I took up my post in the September of 1971. I was keen and enthusiastic and ready to revolutionise the world of teaching. Then I met Mrs P.

On the first day of term, three other probationary teachers and myself were shown into Mrs P.'s office. She was a short, rather dumpy woman with wispy black hair twisted up into a French pleat. She was dressed in a sharp, black suit and was wearing the highest stiletto heels I had ever seen. She swung slowly around on her swivel chair, and all the while she fixed us with her piggy little eyes. She was eating muesli out of a cup, and shovelling it into her red lipsticked mouth with a giant spoon.

She didn't introduce herself. She spoke, but only to tell us her rules.

All staff were prohibited to wear boots, short shirts, or red nail varnish. Overalls would be worn as a punishment should the ruling on short skirts be broken. Overalls were to be found in the cookery department, for those who dared to break the rule.

"We must all set examples for these girls to follow," she said.

You are probationary teachers, and therefore are all on a year's trial. If you fail to meet my expectations, then after this year has ended, you will fail your probationary year and will be asked to leave.

7

Every Friday afternoon I shall require your lesson notes for the following week. Please put them on my desk. I also intend to assess your teaching ability and will be popping into your classrooms from time to time."

At this point she turned to the newly qualified music teacher who was standing next to me. "You will play the piano in assembly. Assembly times are posted on the wall in the staffroom.

About the school. This school is classed as one of 'Special Difficulty'. And for this you have a wage allowance. 'Special Difficulty' also means that we have a lot of problems. This is a multicultural school and we do tend to have a lot of racial tension between the girls. At the last count we had thirty-six different religions. School dinners are a nightmare! Any questions?"

We were shocked into silence.

"Good. In that case we shall meet the rest of the staff."

On the way to the staffroom we passed four senior pupils who were literally standing guard at the front entrance to the school.

"These are my troubleshooters. It's quite common to get dissatisfied or irate parents trying to enter the school. I make sure that I keep a rota of senior pupils ready to fetch me, or one of my senior staff should an emergency arise.

I should be lying if I told you that this was an easy school to teach in. We do tend to get quite a high turnover of staff. It's a tough school. On a positive note, it is invaluable training for you young people. I'll call a meeting so you can meet the others."

'What have I come to?' I thought. The little mouse of a music teacher was nearly in tears.

First Impressions

We were shown into the staffroom where the teachers almost jumped to attention at the arrival of Mrs P. They seemed a cowed, subservient, and down-trodden lot.

She introduced them in turn. The deputy head was a woman called Miss S who smoked incessantly. I later discovered that her nickname was 'Groucho'. This was due to the fact that when she walked, she stuck her head forward and then stuck her arse straight out behind her, like Groucho Marx. I was later to find out that she played Goering, to Mrs P.'s Hitler.

The head of art turned out to be a good laugh that always had pop music blaring out from her classroom, whilst the children bashed and hammered their clay models into shape. I took an instant dislike to the head of English. What a creep! He crawled and slithered his way into the headmistress' good books. The rest of the staff was incredibly young. I remarked upon this to the bubbly art teacher.

"Oh," she said, "they don't stay for long. You've got to be young and tough to survive here. I'm alright, most kids love art, and they get to listen to the radio. Games teachers do pretty well too. It always seems to be the baddies who are good at games.

We have a few off sick with their nerves (the word stress hadn't been invented). Stick around long enough and you could be head of department before you're twenty-four!"

It was then that I met Dave. He taught scripture, but under great protest. He had been dragooned into it by the head. He hated it and freely admitted that he didn't know a thing about the subject.

"I'm glad you're here," he said. "Perhaps I can do more of my own subject now." It turned out that he was the other art teacher. "I have been teaching the New Testament to the O-level classes. Do you want to teach the Old?"

"Fine by me," I said "I don't mind which."

"We haven't got many in the exam classes. I think that might have something to do with me. I've got no enthusiasm for it."

Mrs P. Gets Tough

Mrs P. kept her promise. Every Friday the following week's lesson notes had to be on her desk by four o'clock. Friday was also the day on which she passed comments on our teaching abilities.

During the course of the week she would carry out a spot check on us. The children were terrified of her and would stand to attention as she swept into the room. She would impatiently wave them seated, whilst she ensconced herself at the back of the room. She stared at us, only averting her gaze to write comments in her blue, lined exercise book.

Friday's grilling would go something like this:

"Janet, you need to project your voice more."

"Melanie, you need to improve your handwriting on the board. Your words are sloping downwards. Practise in the break next week."

"Coleen, (the poor music teacher) for pity's sake girl show some authority, you're like a bloody mouse squeaking. They're walking all over you." So it went on.

She would call a staff meeting whenever she felt like it. Mid-morning, or early-afternoon, you were expected to drop tools and leave your class in the hands of two of her Rottweilers who guarded the front door. Once she had a captive audience, you could be there for hours. She spoke on trivial matters. Issues that could easily have been left until Thursday's weekly staff meeting. She simply loved the sound of her own voice.

She was also an Anglophile. Every St. George's day she would stand upon the stage in the hall wearing a red, white and blue P.V.C. mac with a huge white rose pinned to the lapel. Red, white and blue wellies (Carnaby Street I think!), a P.V.C. souwester of the same three colours, and all the while she recited 'Home Thoughts from Abroad' by Robert Browning.

"I'll instil some culture into these buggers," she'd storm.

She loved Shakespeare too, and as we were very close to Stratford you could never call the evenings your own.

"'Comedy of Errors' is on at the Globe," she would announce in one of her frequent staff meetings. "I've hired a bus, it will pick you all up from the school gates at 6 o'clock."

It was no use saying that you had made prior arrangements. She had spoken.

When our probationary year was finished, she called all six of us into her office.

"Well," she announced, "You have completed your first year. Five of you have come up to scratch, but I'm sorry Coleen, I'm going to have to fail you. You're far too soft. Try private tuition. One to one, that sort of thing. This type of teaching is hard and tough and it's not for you." So that was it. Callously dismissed in front of everyone. I never saw her again.

3P

I was allotted a tutor group. My first, and very own class of fourteen-year-olds. They were year three and named P after the first letter of my last name. 3P. I couldn't wait to meet them, and as I was soon to find out, they were dying to meet me!

First rule: get in the classroom first, before the children do. Psychologically this gives you the upper hand. You are waiting for them. Enter the room last and you are vulnerable. In this case, they were already seated, and waiting for me.

Children like to lull you into a sense of false security. The first time you meet them they'll be quiet, sometimes they'll be silent throughout the lesson. You come out of the class and think to yourself, 'that was easy.' What you didn't realise was, that they were eying you up. Noting your weaknesses. Deciding if you are a soft touch or someone who won't be messed with. 3P were silent.

I introduced myself and took a good look at them. Except for one white girl, the entire class was black. There were Hindus, Sikhs, and Gudgerati Indians. West Indians and Cypriots.

'Time to mark the register,' I thought. Anything to break the uncomfortable silence. As I looked down the list of names, I noticed that a great many of the Indian girls had the same surname.

"I notice," I said, "that a lot of you, have Kaur as your last name, are you all related?" There were shy nervous giggles from the Sikh girls.

"Kaur, means princess in our language, Miss. We believe that if you tell someone your real last name you give away a part of yourself."

At this remark, one West Indian child with folded arms and a moody look on her face made a disgruntled sound. Phonetically it sounded like Chaw. It was my first encounter with this word, but I was to hear it everyday in some form or another for the next four years. It was only a sound, but it could mean all sorts of things including:

"You can't make me."

"I'm not doing it."

"Do it yourself."

"Get your hands off me!"

In this case it meant, "This kid's talking a load of crap."

I finished the register and then told them a bit about myself. They sat in curious silence and stared at me. After what seemed an eternity the bell rang, and they filed out to eat their break.

It was my playground duty, so I pulled on my coat and went into the playground. I noticed that some of the little Indian girls from my class were huddled together; eating what appeared to be some sort of green vegetable that they dipped in salt.

"Hello, Miss," said one of them.

"What are you eating?" I greeted them cheerily.

"Have a chilli, Miss. You dip it in salt first like this." She demonstrated.

"I'll have a go," I said. Never having seen a chilli in my life. Walter Simon's grocery shop didn't do exotic.

I bit into it with gusto. I howled. I screamed, and all the while I gasped for water.

The girls roared with laughter. They left me to my plight, with tears rolling down my cheeks. An experienced member of staff approached me, and told me to run into the kitchen and get a piece of dry bread. She sent a kid with me, as I couldn't speak.

After I had composed myself, I reflected on the incident. 'The b******s,' I thought. I had an awful lot to learn.

Battle Won

I eventually won the battle with 3P and became very fond of them. They could be moody and cheeky at times, but on the whole they were alright, especially after I had mastered their swear words. They would mutter strange sounds every now and then. Words that I didn't understand.

"Razclat, blowcla woman!"

I asked a member of staff the meaning of them.

"The little swines," he said. "They are telling you to f*** off in Patois."

'Are they now?' I thought. 'I'll be ready for them the next time.' It didn't take long before the next opportunity arose. This was the early seventies when teachers were into physical violence.

I gave the culprit a swift wang around the ear and said triumphantly, "I'm learning. Progress is slow, but I'm getting there." They didn't try it again.

I was accepted by them and we had a lot of fun in the four years I was there. I also taught drama throughout the school, and we put on some memorable plays and concerts.

One girl's theatrical ability stood out, way and above anyone else's in the class. Francesca Turner was a great actress and an even greater singer. Unbeknown to us all, she would have a glittering career in front of her, for she was to become the great soul singer and diva, Ruby Turner.

The Religious Education Syllabus

I set about improving the standard of teaching in the R.E. department. Class numbers had dwindled so badly that there were only three girls in the O-level class. My efforts were rewarded, and in a very short time, I had a class of ten. Dave undertook the teaching of the New Testament and I continued with the Old.

Mrs P. hadn't given us enough lessons that were needed to complete the course properly, so I diligently taught the class before school commenced in the morning and then after school at night.

We eventually finished our part of the syllabus with only a few days to go to the exam.

The morning of the exam arrived and I popped into the room to see how the girls were faring. They looked perplexed, but seemed to be beavering away. I looked at the paper and did a double take. Discuss the prophesies of Jeremiah, followed by a question on Ezekiel! What was this? There should have been questions on 2. Samuel and 1. Kings. 'They've sent the wrong questions,' I muttered to myself.

I left the invigilating room and went to find Dave.

"The board's sent the wrong questions," I said, and informed him of the situation.

"That's right," he said.

"What do you mean it's right?" I said.

He went white. "The New Testament stays the same, but the Old changes every year."

I had kept on with the same syllabus as last year! I felt sick.

"You didn't tell me!" I wailed.

"I forgot," he said, and then covering himself he added, "And you didn't ask. What the f*** is She going to say?" he said, colour draining from his cheeks.

"We'll ring the board and tell them what we've done. They'll pass them coz it's not the kids' fault."

We tried to adopt an air of confidence as we strode into the secretary's office. She was a horrible old bat, who scraped and grovelled at the feet of Mrs P.

"Can we have the number of the board please?" I asked.

"Why?" she asked suspiciously, narrowing her eyes as she did so.

"We would like to query one of the questions," I said nonchalantly.

I rang the board to explain matters, whilst Dave looked over my shoulder. However, we had forgotten about the old witch, who had ears like 'Jodrell Bank'. She was listening in to our conversation.

The next moment the door was pushed violently open, and there stood an apoplectic Mrs P.

"Staff meeting now!" she boomed. She called all the staff together and motioned to Dave and I to stand in the middle of the room.

She waited until we were all assembled before announcing dramatically, "See these two dull b******s. They have only gone and done the wrong syllabus!"

There was a gasp from the assembled staff and murmurs of;

"That nearly happened to me once."

"What a nightmare!" etc.

We stood with our heads bowed.

"This comes of not communicating with one another. She's ballsed this up, but you're to blame too for not telling her. What a sodding mess! Well, I'll just have to ring the board. God knows what they'll bloody say."

While all this was unfolding, an unsuspecting class of students were still working away at their papers.

After what seemed to be an eternity, Mrs P. returned.

"You two are bloody lucky," she said. "They have decided to give them the benefit of the doubt, and pass them."

I waited until the girls came out of the exam.

"Cor, Miss, it was hard," they said. They had not really sussed out the problem.

I was lucky. They were all Seventh Day Adventists, a strict sect, who spent most of their spare time either in church, or reading their bibles. They were not unfamiliar with the teachings of Ezekiel and Jeremiah. They would not be telling their parents.

They all passed. However the strange thing was, that they wouldn't have had a cat in hell's chance of doing so if they had been sent the correct papers. They were lovely kids, but they didn't have much upstairs!

Time I Went!

Teaching in this particular part of the Midlands was great experience for a young teacher, but there came a time when I decided to move on. I wanted somewhere less frantic and fraught, and as it happened, free from danger.

For example, in 1971 the school experienced at first hand the frightening 'Black Power Gangs'. They were fighting for the freedom of Angela Davis, an outspoken black woman from Birmingham, Alabama, who had been imprisoned for inciting race riots in America.

On one particular day, not long after I had taken up my post, three 'Black Power' gang members, complete with raised, black gloved fists, stormed our school ready to take hostages, and to use violence if necessary. They pushed their way past the 'guards' at the front door and into Mrs P.'s office. It was lunchtime and, as was her wont, she was eating her muesli from a cup.

She looked up at them and said in a calm and cool voice, "Can I help you gentlemen?" and all the while she pushed the panic button underneath her seat with the heel of her stiletto.

The men were nonplussed and just stood where they were, not knowing what to do next. The police arrived in minutes and carted them away.

She returned to her cup of muesli, irritated by the interruption.

Secondly, in 1974, I almost became a casualty of the 'Birmingham Bombings'!

In November 1974, two bombs were placed in two central Birmingham pubs. One was called the 'Mulberry Bush', the other, the 'Tavern in the Town'. One hundred and eighty-two people were injured and twenty-one killed, including two brothers of one of our children. The killings were credited to the Provincial I.R.A. Six men were imprisoned for these atrocities and became known as the 'Birmingham Six'. They were released in 1991 when new evidence proving their innocence was brought in.

The point was that I was in the 'Tavern in The Town' at seven o'clock and the bomb went off at eight.

I thought on. Race riots, bombings, and the fact that I was fiashed at three times in one week, (once at eight in the morning), made up my mind.

I wanted to teach in Shropshire. I had a boyfriend who lived there, and I fancied the laid back way of life. I decided to leave. The trouble was, I had to find a job first.

A Day Out

1975 saw me still teaching in the Midlands, but I had decided to leave at the end of the year. I began to apply for jobs in North Shropshire.

'I ought to get myself a fiat in the area whilst I am searching,' I thought to myself. At this point, I saw an advert in the Shrophire Star advertising a bungalow at a very reasonable rent. I decided to take a look at it.

I loved the little house as soon as I saw it. It was situated in the middle of the owner's lovely cottage garden. His son-in-law had only just finished building it. It was perfect. A lovely kitchen-cum-sitting room, decent sized bathroom with an efficient shower and a bedroom with French windows. I took it.

The owner was a great bloke who turned out to be a teacher himself. He taught at the local boy's grammar school. I told him where I was teaching and that I was looking for a job in the area.

"I'm sure we want an English teacher," he said. He fished out a back copy of the Star and showed me the ad.

"We're a boy's school. Never had women on the staff. We're very traditional and set in our ways."

Undeterred, I asked him for more information and discovered that not only was it a boy's school, but it was also a top grammar school. They only accepted boys with the very best eleven-plus results. No chance for me who was teaching in a rough girl's secondary modern. Well nothing ventured nothing gained. I decided to apply.

I filled in the application form posted to me by the school and thought no more about it, until one day a letter dropped through my door inviting me to attend an interview at the said school.

'It will be a day out if nothing else, and a chance to see how the other half live,' I thought to myself. I decided to go.

It was the summer of '76, and what we now call 'the year of the drought'. The day I was called for interview was a boiling hot one. I arrived at the school early.

It was a very old stone building with ancient windows that you opened by pulling down on ropes. The school even had a quadrangle. I loved it. It reminded me of 'Billy Bunter' books and the film 'Goodbye Mr Chips'. It was in fact a state school, but in stark contrast to my school which was built in the 60's.

I tapped gingerly on the headmaster's door.

"Come!" a booming voice summoned.

I explained who I was.

"Splendid," he said. "Take a seat next to the other candidates. We still have two more applicants to come."

The other two interviewees arrived shortly after me, and I noticed immediately that I was the only woman applicant. I didn't feel nervous. I knew I was the token female and only there to make up the numbers.

The head ushered us into his study and explained that because the weather was so exceptionally warm, and the school far too hot and stuffy, the interviews would be conducted on the cricket pitch!

He swept out of his office and, beckoning us to follow, led us onto the pitch where two tables with chairs had been placed. I was desperately trying to suppress the laughter that was bubbling up in my stomach. All that was going through my mind was that scene in Monty Python where John Cleese sits naked behind a table in the middle of nowhere and utters those immortal lines, "And now for something completely different".

The Interview

The head of English and the deputy head joined us on the field and were introduced to us. The deputy, was a man who was in his late fifties, or early sixties. He had a very unfortunate surname. To these Salopians, his name meant nothing, but in the Midlands where I had just come from, it was a coarse name for a part of a woman's anatomy. I thought that I should explode with uncontrollable mirth!

'Please God, don't let me show myself up,' I begged.

The head of English turned out to be a Welshman from Swansea. He was a powerfully built man who looked like he wouldn't stand any nonsense.

The headmaster briefed us on procedure.

"Mr M. (deputy head) and myself, will interview one candidate at a time out here on the wicket, whilst Mr D. will show the rest of you around the school."

The tour began. We passed through the main corridor which housed a table covered in sports trophies. English schools football trophies, Victor Ludorums. A whole host of impressive sporting achievements on the field.

"No rugby trophies?" I asked Welsh Mr D. He looked at me properly for the first time that day. Indeed, he scrutinised me.

"Are you Welsh, girl?"

"Yes"

"Which part?"

"Pembrokeshire."

"Anywhere near Laugharne?"

"Not far."

"Ah, Dylan country." He waxed lyrical. "I was born in Cwmdonkin Drive, and he was born at No. 5."

"Are you familiar with Under Milk Wood?"

"Yes"

He recited some lines, and quite by chance I was able to quote the lines that followed. From then on the other English candidates were past history.

He moved on to a popular play of the 1970's.

"Have you read Zigger-Zagger?" he asked expectantly.

"Of course," I lied.

I had realised by this time that he loved to talk about himself and all his achievements, which was great for me because he would ask a question, then answer it himself. All I had to say was 'Yes' or 'No' in the right places. I had weaved a complete web of lies without really meaning to. I heard myself saying that I had taught English to examination standard, whereas in reality had only taught it to the special needs class! Still, it didn't matter, I was enjoying myself, and I was only here for the day.

We finally returned to the cricket pitch and to the surreal interview. I was very relaxed. Shame I'd got to leave all this behind and return to my school and its frantic way of life. How lovely it would be to stay here and teach in these idyllic and old fashioned surroundings.

It was now my turn to be interviewed. The head began to ask me some pertinent questions.

"How would you cope with having to discipline a class of fourteen-year-old boys?"

I explained the type of child that we were used to dealing with in the Midlands. I would have no problems on that score.

"How would I cope with an all male staff?"

I answered all their questions, in a laid back and humorous way, and at last the interview drew to a close. 'That was that then,' I thought.

We all had to await the headmaster's decision before we could leave. Finally the head came into the staffroom to inform us (five men and myself) of his decision.

"Would you care to come with us please, Miss Phillips?"

"What for?"

"We should like to offer you the job."

"Me!" I said, looking terrified and slack-jawed.

"Yes, it's about time we had a female member of staff. Bring us into the twentieth century. I am sure the boys will welcome and respect a female member of staff. We were also impressed with your ability to cope in difficult situations as you seem to have done in your present school. Will you accept the appointment?"

"Thank you very much," I said.

What had I done? Told a load of old crap and lies about my examination work in English and now it had backfired on me.

"Come with me," the head of English said, "And I'll let you borrow all the set books you'll need for your classes in September."

He threw me copies of Macbeth, Zigger-Zagger, Brighton Rock and Waiting for Godot.

I was petrified. How the hell was I going to cope?

"Of course, I shall teach the third O-level set," Mr D. said. "As you're our first lady member of staff, we must give you the top set."

"No!" I almost screamed. "I'll have the bottom set. I'm used to teaching them."

"Oh, we've no bottom sets here, just degrees of sound ability. The top set will be yours."

'Shit! Shit! What am I going to do?' I thought.

And so it was that I returned to Birmingham loaded down with classical literature. All to be read and understood by September!

The First Day

All through that boiling hot summer I sweated and toiled over those set books. I even went to see Macbeth in Pembroke Castle.

Finally, the first day of term arrived. My pleasant landlord offered to give me a lift to school each day.

Once at the school, I took a deep breath and entered the hall for morning assembly. The male staff all wore gowns! I stood out like a sore thumb.

The head entered and swept onto the podium. After the usual hymns and prayers, he introduced me.

Every head turned to face me.

"She's a woman!"

"I wonder who's going to be her tutor group?" Sniggers and titters, before they were drawn sharply to order.

"Miss Phillips is our first full-time female member of staff. You will treat her with the utmost respect. Is that clear?"

"Yes, Sir," they all chorused.

The assembly concluded with the hymn 'Jerusalem'. This turned out to be the school song and had been sung for many years. The boys were very proud of it and sang it with great gusto. The beautifully printed verses formed a wide border, which ran along the length of the hall. Assembly concluded, we all trooped off to our classes for registration.

I had been allotted a tutor group. They were fourteen years of age and were called 3W.

"Hello everybody." I called out cheerily.

"Hello, Miss." Titter, titter.

I decided to mark the register. There were a great many Joneses, Williams, etc.

After I had done this I decided to ask them their Christian names, because the names on the roll simply referred to them as Jones S. or where there were two Joneses, a second initial had been added. So you got Jones J.C. or Jones A.F.

"What's your Christian name Jones S?" I enquired.

To my amazement, he became terribly embarrassed. The other boys swivelled around in their chairs to stare at him, waiting expectantly for his reply.

"What's the matter?" I asked.

"We don't know each other's first names, Miss."

'How archaic,' I thought.

Registration over, it was time to meet the brain boxes from year five.

They were such huge tall boys. Every one of them towered above me. I explained a little about the reading material we would be studying for O-level, and as I doled out their books, I once again told them a little bit about myself and where I had previously taught. They stared at me. I was a curiosity, an alien being in a man's world. I was very glad when the bell rang and they all trooped out.

It was time for break. I timidly entered the staffroom and waited for everybody to take their seats. The first rule of teaching practice had been drummed into us. Don't sit in anybody's seat. Some of the old buffers had sat in the same seat for nearly forty years! I sat next to a bloke called Chris who was also in the English department and had secured a teaching position in the school a little before me. He'd got the job even after he had told the board of governors that the whole school smelt of farts! (It was the polish they used). We were both newcomers, so it was inevitable that we became friendly. We talked amongst ourselves.

"I've got a free next," I told him.

"And me".

"I'm dying to go to the toilet," I said, "but there isn't a ladies."

"There's the secretary's lav across the playground," he volunteered.

"I'm not walking all the way over there."

"The headmaster's bog is next door. After break, you go in and I'll keep guard."

"Alright," I said, with some trepidation.

The bell rang and the staffroom emptied.

"Now's ya chance," he said.

As I sneaked towards the head's door, the swine called after me, "watch out for fanny snares!"

I crept in and found a huge, wooden-seated toilet, standing in splendid isolation at the end of the room. The seat was up. I snatched at it to bring it down, but it must have been on a tight spring, because it shot back up, making a loud bang as it hit the wall. I was so desperate to pee that I didn't care, and when I had finished, I opened the door. To my horror the head was standing outside waiting for me to come out.

"What do you think you're doing Miss Phillips?" he asked.

"I had nowhere to go headmaster. I was desperate. I couldn't make it across the playground."

He glanced sharply towards the floor, but not before I noticed the smile that was playing about his thin lips.

"Very well, you may use my toilet in future, but I don't want it filled with female accoutrements, understand?"

"Yes. Thanks very much," I grovelled. Progress had been made. I now had a bog to call my own!

Next lesson up was English with year four. Oh what a difference! These were no young gentlemen. They set out to shock from the outset. I waited for the first coarse jibe. I didn't have to wait long. Sure enough, as I turned to write upon the highest blackboard I had ever seen, one of them let rip with an almighty fart. This was the signal for all of them to collapse and roll around with helpless laughter. I laughed too, I couldn't help it. It was such a beauty. They hadn't planned on this reaction from me and subsequently were bitterly disappointed.

"Who did that?" I asked. Oh, this was better. Indignation, followed by a possible confrontation? This was more like it.

"I did," this burly, dishevelled youth said, proudly, and with a look which said, 'and what are you going to do about it?'

He looked around the class for applause, which of course he got, in bucketfuls.

"What's your name lad?" (No boys in Shropshire, only lads.)

"Morgan"

"Well Morgan, there's funny, you talk with your teeth out!"

Everyone laughed, and suddenly he was the victim. He glowered at me. Obviously this one was going to be a complex nut to crack!

R.E. Lesson With A Difference

After a fraught first morning, it was time for dinner. The staff tables ran along one side of the dinner hall and faced each other. I duly took my faggots and peas and sat opposite a small, shaky little man with thinning, powdery, greasy hair. He turned out to be the chemistry master. He nodded politely to me, but I noticed that he kept looking nervously towards the canteen entrance.

Soon, all became clear, as through the door came this tiny, dapper man. Everything about him was immaculate, including his perfect manners. Just as I was about to tuck into my dinner, this dainty manikin positioned himself behind my chair and tapped me lightly on the shoulder.

"Excuse me my dear," he said. "I have sat in that seat for thirty-three years, do you mind moving?"

Although he was minute, he had a presence about him, so with no more ado, I moved.

It materialised that he was the physics master, and no one, but no one, messed with him, from the gobby deputy head, right down to the most obnoxious of stroppy boys.

Dinner over, it was back to lessons and the testing year four. The lesson this time was religious education. I seated myself at the massive rostrum and opened the heavy, illustrated, leather bound Bible. To capture their attention and interest I intended to read and re-inact something gory from the Old Testament. I had chosen the death of Queen Jezebel, whose body was hurled from her bedroom window onto the hard ground beneath, where it was eaten by a pack of wild dogs. I opened the Bible and asked them to turn to the relevant chapter in their books. Suddenly I was aware of a disturbance, followed by a lot of guffawing. The noise was emulating from the back of the room. I decided to investigate.

I walked to the back of the class and glanced over to where the noise was coming from. A boy called Thomas was fumbling and 'furkling' about underneath his desk. Some of the boys in the immediate vicinity were laughing, others were blushing, whilst the remainder of them looked on, horrified. I wasn't daft and I almost certainly hadn't come down with the last shower of rain. I returned to the teacher's desk and picked up my heavy Bible. The boy called Thomas was still fumbling around under the desk. It was as I suspected. Someone had dared him to wave his willy about, hoping that having witnessed this obscene act, I would then run crying and screaming out of the room, never to return. In his dreams!

I sneaked up behind him and, still wielding the Bible, kicked his desk to one side, thereby exposing him in more ways than one. This done, I brought the massive tome down, WALLOP, right on top of his 'Old Boy'!

"Put it away, Thomas!" I barked. "They do say that too much of that can make you go blind."

He felt foolish and embarrassed. Everyone

sniggered behind their hands and watched as he adjusted his trousers.

"Turn to 2 Kings, chapter nine, and let's have no more nonsense. You can't embarrass me. You're wasting your time and mine. Now can we please get on with some work?"

And so we did.

A Lack Of Resources

The weeks passed and the boys seemed to have settled themselves down. I think that they had realised to their dismay, that to try and shock me was futile.

I needed more exercise books for year two and approached my mate Chris, as to where I should go to obtain the necessary stationery.

"Oh that's Squirrel's department," he laughed. "You'll have to ask him."

"Why do you call him Squirrel?" I asked.

"Because he hoards away the stock like a squirrel with his nuts. You'll have to sign his book if you need a new pencil or a red pen!"

"I don't believe you," I said.

"You'll find out."

Mr P. was a small, pinched little man with pasty, papery skin. It was rumoured that he took an average of sixty vitamin tablets per day. He was into all the latest health kicks and fads, and tried out every new homeopathic remedy that came onto the market. It didn't seem to have done him much good because he looked like a death's head.

He was unmarried and looked after his aged parents. He was in charge of stock and guarded every rubber, pencil and ruler as if it was his own personal booty. He taught French and made sure that each poor kid had used up every conceivable inch of his 'cahir de Francais' before he would issue him another one. He used to scour each page to see if he could find a small usable space.

He was the same with exam papers. There was a story that one particular paper had instructions at the top of the page that said, 'Answer all the questions on the paper.' Apparently he had taken this quite literally and refused to issue any more. The poor boys were writing upside down and in the margins in their futile attempts to answer all the questions.

He never rushed. Every piece of homework was meticulously corrected and checked. The kids took the mick out of him and called him 'Nutkin' to his face, but nothing seemed to faze him. I went in search of him and found him marking his French books in the staffroom.

"Hiya Mr P.," I smarmed, "Do you think I might have some more exercise books and some pens for year two?"

I had spoken to him on a few occasions and I think he liked me. I talked to him about his parents and his strange health kicks. He seemed to appreciate this. Having said this, he still eyed me with suspicion when it came to the matter of stationery.

"How many do you need?"

"Oh, twenty will do."

"And pens?"

"About ten."

He moved secretively to his dray and closed the stock cupboard door behind him so I couldn't see its precious contents.

"You'll have to sign for them. Do you need a red pen?"

I couldn't believe my ears. "Yes, I could do with another one, if you don't mind."

"Here, take this," he whispered, conspiratorially, "And don't tell the others."

"I won't," I promised.

I was carrying my ill-gotten gains along the main corridor when I met Chris.

His eyes opened wide. "Where did you get those from?" he said.

"I raided the dray," I beamed.

Lacking Good Material

Stock, or the lack of it, had become a bugbear. There were of course the exercise books, which had to be prised from the Squirrel's grasp, and then there were the text books. Every department had its own stock cupboard, but some subjects needed more stock than others.

You couldn't, for example, compare the needs of a Latin master with those of an English teacher. The English text books were very tatty and you were lucky if you could get fifteen decent books to go around a class of thirty kids. Also, as I soon found out, you had to bag your reading books at the very beginning of term or you were left with the crap.

No one had told me this, consequently when I went to collect a set of Tom Sawyer for the first years, I found that all that was left in the cupboard was a mangy assortment of Swallows and Amazons! Also, my set of Brighton Rock had disappeared and I was left to teach Tess of the D'Urbervilles to year four, of all classes!

"This is a girl's book, Miss!" They folded their arms sulkily and kicked their desks in disgust.

"It's not really a girl's book. There's a hanging and a rape in it. The Victorians had it banned, because of its lurid material."

Oh, this was better. This would pacify them for the time being.

The serious eggheads in year five were supposed to study Lord of the Flies, but Chris had nicked this and so I was left with The Inheritors, which is a relatively unknown work by Golding.

Tess became a bit of a disaster. I loved it, but they were right, it is essentially a woman's book.

"When's the rape scene coming up, Miss?"

"It's in the next chapter."

An air of expectancy filled the room, as I read from the book. Of course the chapter ends with Alec D'Urberville just about to rape Tess and the rest is left to the imagination of the reader.

"Is that it?" they bawled in disgust.

"Well, it was considered shocking in Victorian times."

"You said that she was raped."

"She was."

"Well where is it then?"

"You must remember," I said, "that this was a puritanical age. Unsavoury things weren't mentioned. Piano legs were draped with material in case they should cause offence and bodily functions, well they were never mentioned. They were all swept under the carpet."

I suddenly realised what I had just said, and so did they. We laughed until we ached. Suddenly, the thought of reading Tess didn't seem to be too bad after all!

On the other hand, Golding's Inheritors was a nightmare to teach. The trouble with the book was that it concerned itself with Neanderthal man and his desperate struggle to survive against the more powerful Cro-Magnon man. Unfortunately both tribes had very limited vocabulary, so consequently when they came across some inanimate object that they did not recognise, they did not have a word to describe it. Primitive man didn't recognise what he was seeing, which also proved very difficult for us, the readers, because we didn't know either. We came across great chunks of text where Golding had just left a question mark. It was quite incomprehensible.

Endless debates ensued as to what the author meant, but to no valid conclusion.

"Right boys," I announced one day, "I'm going to write to William Golding and find out."

"Will he answer?" they wanted to know.

"Well, there's only one way to find out."

I told my head of department what I intended to do.

"He won't answer you. He's a recluse. I wrote to him once and he didn't bother to reply. One must expect it I suppose," he pontificated. "He did win the Nobel Prize for literature."

"I only want to ask him a couple of questions about The Inheritors."

"Carry on, but you're wasting your time."

I wrote to him. I explained that my class of students were reading his book, The Inheritors for O-level and could he explain the missing text to us. Please.

To my utter amazement, and the annoyance of my boss, he replied by return of post. He wrote of the struggle between Neanderthal and Cro-

Magnon man, and that the absence of text didn't really matter. The book concerned itself with man's inhumanity to man. So far so good. He concluded by saying that he had written the book over twenty-five years ago and he had forgotten what most of it was about!

We were studying his work for O-level, and this doddery old bugger couldn't even remember the plot! After this revelation we just made everything up and ended our findings with, 'this has been verified and confirmed by Golding!'

I still have his letter written in his own sprawling hand. I expect it's worth something today!

The C.C.F.

The school had a C.C.F., which stands for Combined Cadet Force. I hadn't ever seen anything like this before, and haven't seen anything like it since. C.C.F.'S are usually commonplace in public schools, but they are a rarity in state schools. The role of the C.C.F. (and I quote) is to 'develop powers of leadership though training, which in turn promotes qualities of responsibility, resourcefulness and endurance through perseverance. Thereby giving service and benefit to the community.'

The art teacher, a young rebel who abhorred war and violence, often refused permission for the boys in his class to attend drill, which was held in the playground every Friday morning at nine prompt. This led to many 'run-ins' with the head. The boys didn't mind missing drill, as they loved art. They adored him, because he really was an excellent teacher. Besides, he allowed them to listen to Radio Luxembourg and to eat sweets in class. He believed that the combination of both enhanced their concentration, and he was right.

However, not even he was exempt from their cruel wit. He was nicknamed 'Johnny Armpit' by the boys because he stank of B.O. and never changed his clothes.

As for the drill, it was hilarious for an outsider to watch the immature male members of staff playing soldiers. They lined the boys up in the playground, where their kit, nails and general appearance was inspected. Joining the forces was supposed to be optional, but any boy who didn't was either considered to be poncey or a trouble-maker. Those who didn't join weren't guaranteed a good school reference because their character was called into question.

The staff were kitted out in full regalia and addressed each other in a manner that befitted their rank.

My landlord was a superior officer in the R.A.F. and was addressed as Wing Commander P. The geography master, (the most childish man I have ever met) was Major R., and the maths master was Captain M.

Drill finished and completed the boys would then return to lessons. We knew when they had finished drill because we could hear them coming along the corridors slipping and sliding in their tacky boots. They would then have to sit through lessons dressed in this garb until break, and only then were the poor souls allowed to return to their school uniforms.

The Crazy Maths Department

When I ever told anyone that I taught in a boy's school and that I was the only female member of staff, the response was always the same, "Oh, lucky you!" This couldn't be further from the truth. To me they seemed ancient, and indeed most of them were. Admittedly one of the games masters was the same age as me, but he was a poser and as dull as a brush. There was the young history master, but he was terribly shy and Chris, who was married. All the others had been there for so long, that you could have dusted the cobwebs off them.

There were strange, fusty old codgers in all of the departments, but none were as odd as the weirdos who taught maths. The head of maths was also one of the senior masters and was quite literally a psychopath who should never have been allowed anywhere near kids. The boys referred to him simply as H. They were terrified of him, but at the same time he amused them, because when he wasn't beating the crap out of them he was making them laugh. The trouble was, you were never quite sure which mood he was in, or whether he was serious or not.

His bulging eyes were the direct result of an untreated over-active thyroid gland. The outcome was that he was either manically hyperactive or completely lifeless and drained. Either way, he was petrifying.

He had no time for me and told me in no uncertain terms that he was strongly opposed to having a female member of staff, and if it had been up to him, I would never have been appointed. When I asked him why, he declared that firstly, the male members of staff could no longer change for games in the staffroom. This sentiment was echoed by the dictatorial and humourless head of games, who was so decrepit that he'd been a 'pathfinder' in the war!

H. also objected to the fact that he had to mind his language now that there was a female on the staff. Thirdly, he pontificated that women did not have the required disciplinary powers needed when dealing with adolescent boys.

I retorted, that firstly, I had seen him and the P.E. teacher changing in the staffroom, and quite frankly they could carry on regardless as far as I was concerned, because neither of them had anything worth seeing.

Secondly, they could swear as much as they liked, it didn't bother me. Lastly, I could certainly discipline children just as well as them, if not better. I added that I had taught in an area which was considered to be the most deprived and toughest part of Britain, whilst they had only ever had experience of the one school. They also had the added advantage and privilege to teach pupils who were clever and who wanted to learn. After this tirade, he and the stringy old games master virtually ignored me for the next four years. Strangely enough though, when I left, he gave me a glowing reference, which I hadn't asked for. It says, 'Miss Phillips does not suffer fools gladly'. I still have it.

To give him his due, he had a brilliant mathematical brain. However, he was only ever interested in those boys who were very adept at maths. Woe betide the poor student who failed to grasp the concept first time. They were ridiculed and lambasted. He was greatly responsible for giving many a boy a complex and a hang up about maths.

He ran quite a thriving little market gardening business outside of school. This was mainly due to the fact that he grew the tomato plants in his classroom and got the boys to tend them.

He was subject to violent and apoplectic outbursts of rage, often for no reason at all. I was witness to this first hand.

This particular day, H. rounded the corner leading to the main corridor and happened upon a class of pupils waiting for their master to arrive for their lesson. The teacher was Mr P. who was renowned for his lateness. The boisterous boys left to their own devices were having a great time, whooping and generally messing about in the corridor, when suddenly one of them set off a firework.

H. demanded to know who had done it and immediately exploded into one of his violent rages. None of them would own up, so he decided to keep the whole lot of them in after school. Now to do this it was mandatory for him to inform their parents of his actions, as some of them lived about two or three miles out of town. He didn't do it. Not only did he keep them in detention, but he also decided to cane each and every one of them.

Whilst they were all bending over with H. whacking each one in turn, an irate parent came storming down the corridor.

"Get your hands off my boy!" he bellowed. "Who gave you permission to keep him in anyway? I'll report you."

As the chap turned to march off down the corridor to find the head, H. stormed up behind him and caned him as well!

As always, he wormed his way out of the situation by grovelling and snivelling to the head.

Second in the maths department was a little man called T. He was quite pleasant, however his mind was everywhere except on teaching maths. He lived and breathed cricket, football and rugby. He looked forward all year to his free skiing trip, when he and the childish geography master took a party of boys to the Spanish Pyrenees. He taught very little. All he did all day was sit on top of his desk and talk sport with the boys. Naturally they didn't object because they weren't doing any work.

T. had a second occupation. It seems so weird looking back on this and quite unbelievable, but it is perfectly true. His sister had the dubious honour of being the only lady undertaker in England. However, sometimes the work became too strenuous for her and so, when she found herself in an awkward, or difficult situation, she would ring the school to engage the assistance of T. At times like these the head would tap on his door and summon him to the phone.

T. would then leave his class unattended and ask the head's permission to attend the dead body. I remember on one occasion, just before lunch, when he was called to the railway line 'to bag up' as he called it, a suicide. When he returned, he sat down to his lunch and gleefully regaled us with tales of bits of brain which he had found on the track and how the poor sod's intestines were strewn all over the embankment!

Soon summer was upon us and T. couldn't wait for the cricket season to begin. I was sitting alone in the staffroom one afternoon, marking a pile of English exercise books, when an eighteen-year-old upper sixth boy, by the name of Guy, tapped on the door.

"Hiya, what do you want?" I said.

"Is there another member of staff in the staffroom, Miss?"

"No, I'm by myself."

"I'll come back later," he said and dashed off.

He returned a few minutes later and stood there shuffling his feet.

"What's the matter lad?"

"Is there anyone with you now, Miss?"

"No, and I'm busy, what do you want?"

He took a deep breath and said, "Mr T. wants a cricketer's box." At this particular time in my life, I was not au fait with cricketing equipment. I am now.

"Why didn't you say so?" I said.

I looked around, and on the floor in one corner of the room were H.'s cardboard boxes that he kept for his tomatoes. They came in varying sizes.

"Do you want small, medium or large?"

When I turned around he had gone.

When T. came in for break, I tackled him.

"Why did you send that daft lad Guy on a message?"

"What's wrong with him?" he inquired.

"Well, he said that you wanted a cricketer's box, and when I went to get him one, he disappeared."

"What did you give him?"

"One of H.'s. I asked him if he wanted small, medium or large, and he ran off."

Gales and whoops of laughter rose from the male ranks. T. opened his pigeon hole and produced a hard, codpiece, type of equipment, which he dangled between his thumb and forefinger.

"Let me introduce you to a cricketer's box," he chortled.

The History And Biology Old Boys

The old history master and my landlord who taught biology were great friends. Again, teaching played second fiddle. This time to Freemasonry. They engaged in whispered and earnest conversations about who 'went through' last night. Talk sometimes turned to the 'Grand Worshipful Master', who had made a fine speech at the novice's inauguration ceremony. My landlord was a Grand Master, as well as being a member of twenty other lodges! Here, he shared boozy nights with his fellow Masons, much to the chagrin of his long-suffering wife.

I shared a free lesson with these two old boys, I was very fond of both of them, but they had completely lost touch with reality. They belonged to the 'Goodbye Mr Chips' world. They had never taught outside the grammar school system and had only fleetingly heard of secondary modern children, whom they referred to as, 'those children'. They didn't intend to cause offence by these remarks they just didn't understand that there were children out there in the real world, who had special needs.

They wore gowns, when only the head and his deputy did. When I asked why they wore them, they replied, "To keep up appearances, my dear. Standards are slipping these days."

When they marked their exercise books, the conversation became very odd, and at times extremely funny.

"I don't know what the matter with Jones S. is this term. His work has really 'gawn' off. Just listen to this, and you'll see what I'm driving at. 'Neanderthal man used primitive tools and had rushed mating on the floor.'."

"Good Lord! Well, I can't say that I'm surprised. I was marking Williams J.G.'s biol exam yesterday, and do you know what the idiotic fool had written?"

"Oh, do tell".

"'The Hydra has testicles above its head, and when it walks, it treads on them.' I ask you? As for Price M., I don't know what's got into him. Listen to this.

I asked the question, 'What is the difference between sperm and an egg?' Do you know what he wrote?"

"No."

"'You can't have sperm on toast!'"

"Fool. You see this is where the two-tier system comes into it's own. Some of these lads would be much better off getting a sec. mod. education. Heaven knows, we all need plumbers."

"Oh, I agree wholeheartedly."

They could not see that these clever and quick-witted boys were taking the rise out of them.

"Well, my dear." They turned their attention to me. "We hear that you are settling down very nicely. Boys behaving like gentlemen?"

"Yes, thanks very much."

"We also hear that you're calling the lads by their Christian names, is that true?" asked the head of history.

"Yes."

"Not advisable. Too personal. They'll only take advantage. Besides, it has always been the tradition. Last names only. Best keep it that way, Miss."

The Egghead's Exams

I had been on the staff for nearly a year. Summer was upon us and it was getting mightily close to the date of the Egghead's exam. God, I worried about them! I didn't want to let them down, especially after I had lied at the interview and told falsehoods about having taught English to O-level standard. I was literally sitting the exam with them, but I felt we were now getting somewhere. I had read Wesker's Chicken Soup with Barley, for the first time, and researched the Spanish Civil War. I had coped with Chaucer's Pardoner's Tale.

Actually, learning Chaucer was hilarious and great fun. Once we had grasped the medieval English, with the help of Neville Coghill and his modern translation, we were away. The end of the tale was 'cut', and the boys naturally wanted to know why they didn't have to learn it.

"It's rude," I told them.

"Tell us, Miss."

They had become less starchy and stuffy over the months. It was a matter of having to. They had me for a teacher.

"Well, I'm not really supposed to."

"Oh, go on."

"Well, alright then, but don't tell Mr D."

"We won't," they chorused.

"Loosely translated, it means, that the pardoner

finishes his tale and begins to sell his pardons. He turns to Harry Bailey the host, and says; 'Harry, you have the most sins, so you can come up to the platform first and buy my pardons.'

The host, enraged and humiliated replies, 'I wish I had thy coillons in my hond, I would cut them and roll them in a hogges torde!' Which translates as: 'I wish that I had your balls in my hand, I would cut them off and roll them in pig's shit!'"

Hell, those boys laughed. I had never heard them really laugh before. For days they ran around the quad shouting, "Coillons to you." Funny how kids have no trouble at all when it comes to learning the dirty bits! If only they could have learned Macbeth so well.

How I had sweated over Macbeth. In the 70's, examinations were much more difficult than they are today, and pupils were required to learn context questions, which meant that the students were given a piece of text, and they were supposed to know what preceded it, what came next, who said it and so on.

One week I had set them Macbeth's most famous monologue for their homework.

'She should have died thereafter; There would have been a time for such a word,' right down to, 'It is a tale told by an idiot full of sound and fury signifying nothing.'

"Oh, come on, Miss," they moaned in unison, "That's too much. We'll be up all night."

"Do you want to pass this exam or not?" I demanded to know. I had to learn this very same speech for my O-level English Lit."

"I bet you can't do it now," one of them piped up.

"I'll try. Just give me the first line," I mused.

They recited it. I threw back my head and grasping my forehead betwixt thumb and forefinger pretended to concentrate hard.

"Hold on, I think I have it."

I rattled through it, using all the dramatic gestures that I could muster. When I had finished they all cheered.

"Fancy you remembering that from all that time ago!" they marvelled.

"Here, watch it," I said, "I'm not that much older than you lot."

"Yeh, Yeh." When you're seventeen, twenty-five is ancient.

"So, my desk tomorrow morning, please. If this old 'un can do it, your seventeen-year-old brains should rattle through it!"

After the lesson had finished, I plonked myself down in my teacher's chair and thanked God that things had all gone to plan. I'd been up all night learning that speech!

The day arrived and I couldn't wait to look at the paper. I was so nervous. I wasn't allowed to invigilate because it was my exam, but I could look in on them and take a peep at the paper.

I scanned it quickly. The main context was part of Macbeth's soliloquy. I looked around the room and they all had their heads down and were scribbling away. Just when I was about to leave, I looked at them once more. Morley gave me the thumbs up and laughed. It was all going to be O.K.!

The Skiing Trip

Every February half-term, the school arranged a trip to the Spanish Pyrenees. The same male members of staff went each year. These included the childish geography master, the part-time undertaker from the maths department and the miserable old games teacher. I had never been abroad and I really wanted to go on this trip. I had now been in the school for three years, so I did think that I qualified for a place.

"You haven't got a chance," Chris said. "Those selfish buggers go every year. They've got it all sewn up between them."

"Well, I'm going to ask the head if I can go."

"You're wasting your time," he said.

I knocked on the head's door and waited for the familiar 'Come.'.

"What can I do for you, Miss?" he beamed.

"Can I go on the skiing trip, headmaster?" I pleaded.

"I don't know. Better leave it with me and I'll think about it."

That was that. Think about it. Well that meant no.

A few days later, I was summoned to his office.

"I have been thinking, Miss. It is about time another member of staff had a chance to go on the trip, you can take Mr. A's place."

Hell, that old bugger was mad. "I've been going on this trip for the past ten years," he fumed. "You're not a qualified instructor. You can't ski."

"Tough. I'm going and you're not. So pick the bones out of that and get used to the idea!"

I was so excited and nervous because I had never fiown before. The day arrived. Twenty boys and three members of staff. We were off for the Pyrenees. This was my first school trip, but it turned out to be no picnic!

We arrived at Luton airport in freezing, wet conditions. It materialised that the plane couldn't take off because of ice on the wings. We had to wait four hours before we could board. By this time I was getting really panicky.

The other two men took no notice of me. They were still peeved with me for taking the old 'pathfinders' place. I sat by two lovely-natured boys who were in year three.

"Have you ever fiown before, Miss?" they wanted to know.

"No. What's it like boys?"

"It's O.K. You'll be alright."

We finally took off. The plane bumped and swayed around a lot, but I presumed that was what fiying was all about. We finally landed.

"That was alright," I remarked to the other two members of staff. It was only then that I noticed that they had turned a delicate shade of green.

"That was a terrible fiight." they groaned. "Didn't you see the passengers at the rear of the aircraft being sick?"

"No."

"Couldn't you feel the plane rocking and rolling?"

"Yeh, but I thought that it was normal."

"That's what's termed turbulence," they muttered.

Well ignorance is bliss. I felt fine.

Safely off the other end, we then had to take a hazardous and long coach journey through Basque country. We all had to show our passports and the boys told to be quiet, as these fierce looking men with crossed guns asked us our business, before they allowed us to pass.

We finally arrived at our destination. I thought that it would be a posh hotel. It was more like a youth hostel. Disappointment number one.

For dinner we had boiled potatoes, veal and stewed green peppers. It was vile. The boys moaned too.

The next day was our first day on the slopes. The nursery slopes for all, except for the two men. The Spanish instructors kitted us out in ski boots and attached skis to our feet.

I was so naïve that I just assumed that we walked straight out of our hotel and onto the ski slope. I hadn't realised that we had to reach the slopes using ski lifts. I have a terrible fear of heights and I just froze when I saw these two-seater open chairs, swinging and bobbing their way up to the slopes.

'I can't do this,' I thought. I was really very scared. I had these huge boots on, great long skis and a ski pole in each hand. I grabbed the nice kid who had sat by me on the plane.

"Will you sit next to me, Martin?" I pleaded.

"Sure, Miss."

There was a knack to getting on the thing. It was moving. You looked behind you and positioned yourself like you would if you were going for a pee. Having done this, you were then meant to sail seamlessly onto it and it would take you up to the top.

It hit me behind the knees so hard that my eyes watered. Thank God for Martin, who grabbed me and dumped me into the seat.

"Cor, look down below, Miss!" he exclaimed with wonder. "There's wolf tracks down below us."

I shut my eyes all the way to the top, but now I had to get off the thing, wearing boots, skis and carrying ski poles. I fell off it and really bruised my knees. 'I hate this,' I thought, as I picked my way to the nursery slopes. I was hopeless. I kept falling down and hurting myself. The snow wasn't soft. It was packed ice. I had imagined myself, bowling down past little wooden chalets, full of Heidi-type people, but this was nothing like it. The place was full of Pyrenean mountain dogs 'hecking' around on three legs. Rabies sprang into mind.

After a day of humiliation, I had to descend the mountain via that bloody ski chair again.

I grabbed the nearest kid and said, "Stay here next to me and tell me when we reach the bottom."

The thought of repeating this performance every day gave me a terrible nervous stomach, which resulted in diarrhoea. Over a period of one week, I consumed eighty-eight 'Dia-calm' tablets.

I hated the skiing, the food and most of all the f*****g lift.

The night before we were set to leave, one of the older boys came to me and whispered urgently in my ear.

"Miss, Miss, Terry's been sick. Will you come quick!"

"Ask, Mr M.," I said, "He's on duty."

"Please, Miss. We're too scared to tell him. Will you come?"

They had four bunk beds in their room. I went in and was speechless with horror. The little swines had got hold of some sangria and drunk the lot. The boy called Terry, who occupied the top bunk had been sick and had spewed right through the springs of his mattress and onto the bunk below! There was sick everywhere and we were going home the next day. There was no point shouting at them because they had had their punishment. They were green. Well, there was nothing to be done but to get on with it.

I cleaned the room as best as I could, but I had to inform the management. The boys didn't mind this, as long as I didn't grass them up to the two other members of staff.

The next day we faced a nine-hour journey through the mountains. The four lads vomited for most of the way. The two male staff just thought that they were suffering from travel sickness.

We had to make a detour through France and, due to bad weather, the plane couldn't take off and we had to spend the night sleeping on the airport floor. The authorities apologised for the twenty-four hour delay and gave us chicken and chips. It was the best grub we had in a week.

I was never so glad to see Shropshire. However, just when I thought that things must now pick up and improve, the consequences of devouring eighty-eight 'Dia-calm' tablets caught up with me. I was corked up, and couldn't go to the toilet for nearly a week. Serve me right for wanting to go skiing in the first place.

When I returned to school, the old games master asked me how I had enjoyed myself.

"Oh very good," I lied.

"That's not what I heard," he said. "I heard that you copped the wooden spoon for being the worst skier," he added with glee.

"Oh balls to you!" I fumed, and fiounced off.

The School Closes

I had been in the school for four years and was really enjoying it. However, we were delivered an earth shattering blow when the head called a staff meeting and told us that the school was to close. The boy's secondary modern, the girl's high and us were to amalgamate and become one very large comprehensive. The staff were bereft. Of course, there were some older members of staff who, whilst they were upset to see the school disappear, were also delighted, because it meant that they could claim redundancy money and then take early retirement. They were alright. Then there were staff like Chris and myself, who were not in line for a large payout and were faced with the prospect of a new school and a new job. It was not a welcome prospect.

The sixth form were not to be included in this new regime. The new comprehensive only catered for pupils from eleven to sixteen. They were going to a tertiary college.

I couldn't bear the thought of losing our quad, the old school traditions and our school song. I would even miss the C.C.F. I decided to go back home. Chris was going to teach in the tertiary college. I would miss him.

When it came to the end of the summer term we had a staff photo taken and a full school one to mark the closure.

"What are you going to do, Miss?" asked Ben, one of my favourite pupils.

I decided to make a joke of it.

"I'm not going to teach anymore, Ben," I announced.

"What are you going to do then?"

"I am going to be a professional blackhead squeezer!"

"Ugh!" they chorused.

"No, I'm going home to Wales." And I did. I was very sad to leave.

Many years later I returned to look at the old building. It had been turned into a criminal court. 'Quite fitting,' I thought to myself, since it had been a criminal act to close that lovely old school.

The Big Comp

I returned to Wales and found that teaching jobs back home were very thin on the ground. I took a non- teaching job for a year until my mother chanced to meet a woman in town who was one of the secretaries who worked at the large, local comprehensive.

"There is an English post going at our school, if Mel is interested," she said.

"Are you going to apply for this job in the comp.?" my

mother inquired.

"No."

"Why not?"

"What if I got the job, I would be teaching with staff who had previously taught me. How embarrassing!"

I had been a pupil at this school, but when I was there it was a grammar school with only five hundred kids. Now it was a huge comprehensive with over one thousand pupils. Also many more buildings had been tacked on to it. The whole place was almost unrecognisable to me.

However, I was persuaded to take a look at the job description that was advertised in the local paper. I applied, not caring if I got an interview or not. I walked up to the school with my application form and gave it in at the desk. The headmaster just happened to be in the secretary's office at the time. He started chatting to me and then out of the blue he said, "You can be our final applicant, Miss Phillips." And informed me of the date of the interview. 'How odd,' I thought. 'He hasn't even seen my C.V.'

I duly arrived for interview on the appointed day and discovered that there were three other candidates for interview, two men and one other woman. I was familiar with one of the male candidates and knew that he was very highly qualified, having gained a first class honours degree in English.

I was last to be interviewed and found myself being grilled by the head of English. He was the very man who had taught me at A-level. It was obvious that he didn't rate me at all. The headmaster on the other hand, was extremely friendly and solicitous. I was very relaxed and nonchalant about the whole affair, knowing that the head of English wanted the bloke with the excellent English degree and why not, he was by far the best candidate.

Interviews over, all candidates waited in the staffroom to hear the head announce the name of the lucky interviewee. Eventually he entered the room, and to my jaw dropping surprise, told me that he wanted to offer me the job.

"Thank you," I spluttered.

Later, I had to pick up some forms from the secretary's office and tapped on the door. One of them rushed out and said expectantly, "Did you get the job?"

"Yes," I said.

"I knew it. I told you she'd get it! You lot owe me a fiver." she exclaimed, triumphantly.

Noticing my perplexed face she added, "We had a bet between ourselves."

"And?" I urged.

"Oh, it's the head, the dirty old bugger is a sucker for big knockers."

And I thought that I'd got the position on my own merit. I wasn't sure that I wanted this job!

Term Starts

I arrived early on the first day of term, eager to make a good impression. In the staffroom there were three other members of staff. The old boy that used to teach me history was sitting in one corner of the room looking for all the world as if he had been mummified. He was fast asleep. In the opposite corner were two women. The first was busily divesting herself of her leather biker's gear and was at that moment in the process of removing her helmet and shaking out her long black curly hair.

Sitting opposite her was a woman who looked like she had stepped straight out of Vogue magazine. She was beautifully dressed. I watched in fascination as she dipped her contact lenses into some kind of pink solution and then slid them effortlessly into both eyes. All this, whilst keeping a conversation going with the tall girl in the Hells Angel's gear.

At last they spotted me.

"Oh, hiya," chirped Miss Whiplash. "You're new." They introduced themselves.

"What do you teach?" she asked.

"English," I said.

"So do I!" enthused the immaculate one, whose name turned out to be Jan. Come with me when the bell rings, and I will familiarise you with the

83

other members of the English department. All our classrooms are in A block."

It was a good job she was at hand to guide me, otherwise I should never have found my way. The school was vast, with endless stairs to climb. I was knackered before I had even started.

"You'll get used to it," she laughed. "It's good for the figure. When I first started I lost half a stone in a fortnight! There are four staffrooms so you can take your pick. I wouldn't choose E block staffroom if I were you, that's where he goes for his break."

"Do you mean the head?" I asked.

"Yes. If you fancy being touched up by him that's the place to go."

Horror of horrors. I had come from a sedate and refined pedagogic haven to this depraved hole.

"Personally, I use D block canteen."

We finally trouped into the hall for assembly. I was glad to see that it hadn't changed a bit since I was a kid. The head welcomed everyone back from the summer break and introduced the six brand new members of staff. I recognised the music master from a previous briefing, and remember thinking that he was a grumpy ignorant individual, and glancing across at him today, I had no reason to change my mind.

"Would the new members of staff stay behind after assembly please, I should like to introduce you to your tutor groups."

The rest of the pupils except for our children, were dismissed along with their form tutors, some kids muttering words to this effect; "Oh not her," or, "I 'ate him, why couldn't we have had so and so, he's a good laugh."

Six brand new members of staff were left looking at about one hundred and eighty kids. All of a sudden the music teacher whispered to me, "Sorry about yesterday. You must have thought that I was a right miserable t—t. Truth is that I'd had a sesh at the rugby club the night before and I was feeling bloody awful." I laughed. After this shaky and somewhat uncertain start, Wally, for that was his nickname, and I embarked upon seven years of great laughs, along with a few odd and strange encounters thrown in for good measure.

We were finally allocated our groups. Mine was called 5M1. This translated meant that they were fifth formers and sixteen years of age. M stood for the name of their house and 1 meant that they were alphabetically the first. It certainly didn't mean the first when it came to brains.

I stared at them and they stared at me. It had suddenly dawned upon me that it was the first time in my twelve year teaching career that I had encountered a mixed class. As I marked the register, I found that I was constantly addressing myself to the boys. They must have thought that I was some kind of pervert. It was just that I hadn't seen any girls for four years.

"Does anyone know where Pat Williams is?" I enquired.

"She's got her appointment with the physiatrist today, Miss," squeaked a fat, spotty girl, who was busily digging lumps out of her desk with a decent looking fountain pen.

They must have noticed the look of incomprehension on my face.

"She's bit off part of Donna Simpson's ear, Miss," Spotty explained. "She'll be back saffnoon."

"I see," I said, lamely.

Look After Number One

This school was vast! There were eighteen hundred kids and one hundred and twenty members of staff! It was unworkable. I had only been there about two days when I heard one of the history masters addressing a member of the P.E. staff. He was asking the member of staff in question how he and his family were keeping, because it turned out that he hadn't seen him in six months!

I lost my way in the maze of corridors countless times. There were so many canteens and staffrooms. My base was in A corridor, and was the home of the English department. History was D block, maths E block and so on. All except for the music department. How I envied them. They were tucked away in an old manor house near to the school gardens and woods. Many years previously, presumably in the 19th century, the school, the gardens and farm had all belonged to the lord of the manor. Evidence of this was to be seen in the woods, where there was once a thriving bamboo plantation. Shades of the Raj. The school still retained the farm. It was home to hundreds of smelly turkeys.

I discovered that there were twelve staff in the English department. I already knew the head of English, but as a pupil, not as a member of staff. He had taught me A-level English. He had a brilliant mind and was more highly qualified than the headmaster. He was a Cambridge graduate. I was soon to learn that he treated his staff in the same way he had treated his pupils; just as if they were inferior to him, and of course we were. He had a look which could wither you away and was also possessed of a razor-sharp acerbic wit. With just one word he could make you feel stupid and inadequate.

We soon had our first departmental meeting where we were each allocated our classes. It soon became clear that last in got doled out all the bottom C.S.E. classes. He had bagged all the able and clever kids.

"You promised that I could teach some O-level classes this year Mr Hunt," said Jan, bravely. "You definitely said last term, that now I had been here for five years, I would get some better classes."

"You have got better classes," he snapped. "I have given you the top C.S.E. set."

"But you said that I could have an O-level set. Could you have the top C.S.E. class instead? They are the top," she added, trying to pacify him.

He gave her a dismissive look and said, "Look here my dear, I didn't go to Cambridge to teach those persons!"

And that was that, end of the discussion. To think that in my last school they had insisted I have the top set because I was female and therefore had to be treated with respect.

Staff meeting ended, Jan and I walked off down the main corridor which led to the school exit.

"That old bugger will never share," she said,

bitterly. "Always grabs the top sets and all the examination classes for himself. The head of maths always takes his turn with the tail-enders. See you tomorrow," she called after me.

I couldn't see why she was moaning. I glanced at my list again. C.S.E. six and even an eight! I didn't know C.S.E. went down as low as that!

The Hard Nuts

All of my classes had some redeeming factors about them, but there was nothing to commend any of 3PA. They were indeed a detestable bunch of fourteen-year-olds. They were cheeky and manipulative, and sometimes even violent. A particularly nasty girl and her two pals were the ringleaders of the class. 3PA's claim to fame was that they alone were responsible for sending their maths teacher to the local mental institution. My friend Audrey took them for drama and I would watch her whilst she psyched herself up before entering their classroom. She was lucky, she only had them once a week; I had them for six periods a week for English.

The trick was to constantly keep them entertained. It was exhausting, but I managed it most of the time.

This particular day I had to go to the dentist and told the head that I would be back before lunchtime. In fact I got back around eleven. Our head of English had been detailed off to teach them in my absence. This was the man who had never ever seen a less than able child, let alone come into contact with a whole class full of unruly delinquents.

I peeped unobserved through the panel in the glass door and saw to my horror that he was actually trying to teach these kids Shakespeare! There was absolute pandemonium in the room. I opened the door and all the class cheered.

"Where you been, Miss? This old bloke is so boring."

My boss made a dash for the door and as he was making his hasty exit, he turned to me and said, "How many times a week do you attempt to teach these persons, Miss Phillips?"

"Six," I replied.

"You need a f*****g medal," he called back over his shoulder, as he hotfooted it down the corridor.

One of my senior classes turned out to be likeable rogues, but at times they too could be exasperating. They were fifteen-year-olds, and mainly boys.

I had been there a few weeks and had got to know all their names. I am hopeless with numbers but if I see a class of people, children or adults maybe twice, I can tell you all their names. It is just a weird quirk I have. Ask me someone's telephone number and I will never remember it. I only mention this because I had been in the school for about a week and was about to start the lesson with this group of fourth years when this tall insolent boy strolled into the room.

"Sorry I'm late, Miss," he said, rudely, looking around for applause as he did so. The rest of the class dissolved into stifled laughter.

"You don't belong in this class," I said.

"I do, Miss," he said. He obviously thought that I wouldn't remember all of the class member's names.

"You don't belong here, so go. Now," I said, with authority. He took no notice of me and started laughing and joking with some of the boys. He totally ignored me. I was so angry that I positioned myself behind him and footed him swiftly up the backside with my boot. He staggered forward, but didn't fall. Instead he turned on his heel, and as he went to leave he looked over his shoulder and whined, "I'm not coming in here again, you're Sid Vicious." And so a nickname was born. For ever afterwards I was referred to behind my back, as Sid. They even wrote it on the back of my teacher's chair.

"Sid's chair. Don't touch."

Some of them used to make me laugh so much that even though I tried my best to keep a straight face I found that it was impossible to do so. One day I asked one of them if he was the youngest in his family. Quick as a flash he came back at me with, "No, Miss, the cat's two."

There was also a boy called Paul who was one of the funniest kids I have ever taught. His dad had a smallholding and kept a small number of Welsh Black cattle. He came late to the lesson one morning and announced, "Sorry I'm late, Miss, but the cow 'ave calved. Nice'll thing. She's female, so I thought I'd call her Melanie."

"So you're calling me an old cow are you?" I said, dying to laugh.

"No, Miss, she's quite pretty really," he laughed.

He could make a noise exactly like a cow lowing. If you asked him to do it, he'd say, "I'll do it later." I'd forget all about it and then when you were doing some serious work, or I was reading to them, he would make the cow noise and the whole class including myself could do nothing but collapse into fits of laughter.

Then there was H. He would eat anything, and I mean anything, for a bet. The boys of course had to make it worth his while. He had a sliding scale that he used as a marker for various disgusting things. For five quid he would eat worms and slugs or even crunch up the odd earwig. For more revolting stuff the price rose steeply. I unwittingly witnessed him eating a pile of cow dung from the farm, all mixed together with various unmentionables.

"Look what H. is eating, Miss!" one of them bellowed, as they all entered my classroom.

"What is it?" I asked, not really wanting to know.

"Cow shit, Miss." H. opened his mouth wide in order to verify this.

"Get out! Get out! You vile creature," I screamed, and yet at the same time I was desperately trying to stop myself from laughing.

Year five C.S.E. eight were very different. There was only about twenty of them, but it seemed like there were forty. They were all boys except for one lovely looking girl. I really don't know what she was doing in that set. She was bright and hard working. All the boys were in love with her, but she wanted nothing to do with them, all she wanted to do was to get on with her work. They would all look at her adoringly and sometimes try and sit next to her. She would sigh and utter a wearisome, "Tell um, Miss."

Those boys were awful. You had to keep them entertained perpetually otherwise they would have walked all over you and created mayhem. I used to look forward to the beginning of May when the spud picking started. That was the only time you were guaranteed that they would be absent from school. I would say to them, "Why do you come here?"

"You tells good stories, Miss. We likes that one about the fella who got shot in the 'ead, and the one about the inspector."

They were a strange bunch. They loved Steinbeck's Of Mice and Men, and George Orwell's Animal Farm. The trouble was that a lot of other classes did too. The result was a stock cupboard scrum. I have physically wrestled 'Kes' out of my colleague's hands. The trouble was that Steinbeck's and Hines's books are all rather short, so you would have to read them slowly to eke them out. They also loved J.B. Priestley's play An Inspector Calls. I never knew why this was. It is so dated.

The biggest bully in the class would always want to play the inspector. The problem was that he could hardly read, so you got loud impatient tuts from the rest of them, or cries of, "Give the part to me, Miss, he's useless. He can't read, Miss. He's boring."

"Shut your gob you, right, or I'll smack you one."

And so it would go on. There they would be, these oafish louts of boys, reading dated, upper class and foppish lines in a bumbling and stumbling way, and all delivered in a monotone.

"You bounder, I didn't expect this caddish behaviour from you!"

I didn't dare laugh. They all thought that they were budding Oliviers.

Most of them ended up in Swansea nick when they left school, or at the very least found themselves on the pubs 'behave or be banned list' which is circulated around all public houses in town. I used to read down the list of banned persons and say yes, I taught him and him and so on.

There was one boy in the class who was different from all the other Neanderthals. His name was Martin. He shouldn't have been in the class at all. He was there because he was so bone idle and refused to do any work.

The first time that I met him, he said to me, "Have you got false teeth, Miss?"

"No," I said, looking surprised and very amused.

"I 'ave," he said, and dropped his front teeth down to his bottom lip to demonstrate. "My mam and my gran have too. My nan uses hers to make pretty patterns round the apple tarts she bakes. Shall I bring you in a piece?"

"Go on then," I said. I had learned very quickly over the years, never refuse a gift from them. Whether it be a manky sweet or a grotty, manhandled piece of sponge, they will take it as a personal affront.

"I've got piles too," he added. He said it with a certain pride in his voice. I have to sit on a wooden chair. The plastic ones make my arse sweat."

When I had composed myself, I said, "What about your C.S.E. exam, you'll have to sit on a plastic chair in the hall along with everyone else?"

"I'll get one," he said.

Much later on in the year when it was time for year five to sit their English exam, I was invigilating in the hall. The pupils were obliged to raise their hands if they required more paper. Martin had raised his hand and so I walked towards him with a sheaf of writing paper. I was delighted that he required more. It turned out that he didn't want paper at all. He beckoned me closer to him and pointed at his wooden seat, the only one in a sea of blue plastic chairs.

"I told you I'd get one," he said, triumphantly.

A few years later when I was teaching in a junior school, the door was flung open and this tall, blonde haired young man bounded into my room.

"Hiya kids," he said. "No need to get up, I hope she's treating you all right."

"What do you want Martin? I laughed. "I haven't seen you for ages."

"Just thought I'd come to see how you was getting on. I bet I earns more than you do. I'm a tea boy on the site. Brilliant money."

He told me how much he earned, and it was far in excess of what I took home.

As he was going through the door, he shouted; "Look at this kids." He dropped his front row of teeth down to his chin. The class screamed with delight. "See ya," he called over his shoulder to me.

The Music Department In The Woods

The music department was the envy of all. They were based in an old manor house that was situated on the lower drive. From this vantage point they could easily see if the headmaster was headed their way.

The old head had been very laid back and lazy and never bothered to take a trip down there to check on them. It would have been far too much of an effort for him to walk. However, a new and keen head had been appointed and he made it his business to seek everyone out. He had already caught the rural science teacher, who was tucked out of the way in the school gardens, with his feet up on the desk, puffing away on a fag and reading The Sun newspaper. The music department however, was ever vigilant and had positioned their desks in such a way that they, or the kids, could see him coming.

In this peaceful environment they could do whatever they pleased.

The head of music had a theory that no one ever made a check on the registers at the end of every term. To prove his point he hid his register under the floorboards. He was right. Nobody asked for it, despite it being a legal document. It is probably still sitting there gathering dust today.

There were three members of staff in the department. These included the head, the second in command, a pinched and miserable man devoid of personality, who went on to become a school inspector (say no more) and my friend Wally, the newcomer.

A goodly amount of Wally's monthly salary went over the bar at the local rugby club, leaving him short of such necessities as toilet paper. He overcame this little problem in his own inimitable way.

The forerunner of the photocopier was called a 'Banda' or to give it its proper name, a 'Spirit Duplicator'. The Banda was basically a machine with a roller in the middle and a handle that you turned. A worksheet was typed onto blue carbon paper which had a waxed paper fastened to the back. You typed on the first sheet and the pressure of your typing was transferred onto the spirit master. You always kept your master for further use. You turned the handle until you had the required number of worksheets for your class. It was a filthy process, and when you had finished your hands were covered in ink. You then had to wait for the sheets to dry. Kids loved the Banda. The spirit that was used was toxic and it gave them a high, very much like sniffing glue. This potential hazard eventually signalled the death knoll of the Banda.

When money became tight towards the end of the month, Wally always found that he had no spare cash for toilet paper. Here the Banda came into its own. He would cut the printed sheets into neat little squares and use them as makeshift

Andrex. However, there were two major fiaws to this cunning scheme of his. Firstly he found that his toilet at home became regularly blocked, and secondly there was another unforeseen problem. He arrived at school one day and whispered to me, "I hope I don't have an accident which results in me having to go to hospital."

"Why?" I asked.

"Because I have a treble clef emblazoned right across my arse."

We had been in school for a few months when all talk turned towards the school trips. Most departments had their own trip. All that is, except the English and music departments.

Wally and I decided that we had to go on a trip too. We would wheedle our way onto somebody else's trip. We hadn't bargained for the response and cliché-ness of some members of staff.

"Oh, we're full. We have the same members of staff who go with us every year. Sorry."

Nobody wanted us. Finally, when we thought that all was lost, the head of classics, who was a wonderfully kind and sophisticated woman, allowed us to go on her Latin trip. They were going to Caerleon to see the Roman remains and then onto Cardiff to the city library to do some research.

The kids who were going on the Latin trip were the crème de la crème. Wally and I hadn't encountered children like them in this school before. They were brainy and snobby unlike the kids we taught.

We set off at about half past eight and began the first leg of the journey to Caerleon. We stopped at Cross Hands so that everyone could go to the toilet. In the lay-by there happened to be a burger van.

"I'm going to get myself a burger," Wally announced. "I'm starving."

"Didn't you have any breakfast?" I enquired.

"No. Didn't have time."

He got out and bought himself the biggest, sloppiest looking hamburger I had ever seen. It was so greasy and wet that he decided that it would be best all round if he ate the thing outside the bus.

The children were all waiting inside, everyone that is except him. Suddenly I heard a very well-spoken child say to the friend who was sitting next to her, "Look at him. He's just like a savage."

I thought that I should explode with laughter and when he returned, I told him what the girl had said.

"Snooty little f****r," he sniffed.

On we went until we came to Carleon, our destination.

We all trooped off the bus and were greeted by our guide who was to show us around the remains of the Roman baths. We were all directed to stand in a circle on a low grassy wall. He stood in the middle of the circle with his artefacts and relics.

He talked at length about Roman toilets and how going to the toilet was seen as a social occasion for all. As if this wasn't enough information, he produced a visual aid, a chart that depicted Romans laughing and joking, whilst wiping their arses with a sponge, which was secured onto a stick. He explained that if you didn't like the bloke who was ensconced next to you, you gave him the 'wrong end of the stick'.

Or in this case the 'shitty end of the stick'. He triumphantly explained that this was how we got the idiom that we use today. Fancy giving someone the shitty end of the stick on purpose! When I heard this I laughed so much that I fell off the low wall onto the grass beneath.

Wally was also helpless. To make it worse the same snotty kid was heard to say, "What an example."

On to Cardiff and the city library. The classics teacher announced to all that the staff would see them back at the library at five sharp.

"You two may do as you please," she said us. Wally was delighted.

"Come on, I'll show you a good pub," he enthused. "I went to university in Cardiff."

"Does it sell food?" I said, "I'm starving."

"Yeah, we'll sort that."

I followed meekly. "I can smell the Brains S.A. from here!" he announced, ecstatically.

The pub was called The Bluebell and it was the filthiest pub I had ever seen. Needless to say, it didn't sell food.

"A pint of Brains please mate." he addressed himself to a barman who was wearing a verminous vest and was scratching himself behind the lager pump.

"What'cha want Mel?"

"I'll have a medium dry sherry please," I said, addressing myself to the scratcher.

"What the f***'s that?" he said.

I paid a visit to a toilet that was so disgusting that I found myself hovering over the seat.

We stayed in this vile place until four-thirty, when we eventually bade goodbye to The Bluebell and made our way back to the bus.

"He's drunk," one girl was overheard to say. "What an example to set!"

She was right.

The History Department

Three times a week I was required to teach religious education over at D block. D Block was home to the R.E., history and geography departments.

The head of the history department had taught me when I was in school. He was a man of very strange and ritualistic habits. He had taken possession of an old wooden chair. His Chair. Nobody else was allowed to sit on it. It was positioned in a particular corner of the staffroom. At precisely eight-fifteen every day, he would enter the staffroom and plonk himself down on one of the bog standard plastic orange chairs. Here he would meditate for ten minutes with his hands clasped into a steeple shape, his eyes closed and his legs crossed right over the other, very like Kenny Everett's character Cupid Stunt.

After ten minutes had elapsed, he would jump to his feet and seek out his wooden chair. Once ensconced, he immediately went to sleep for exactly five minutes whilst he waited for his pals to come and join him in the staffroom. Once gathered together they set about putting the world to rights until the bell rang for morning school. The ringing of the bell signalled another move for the chair, this time into another corner of the room ready for break, where he would bore an entirely new set of staff. When the bell rang to signal the end of break, the chair was moved into its dinnertime spot. Here he positioned it so that he had a good view of the young members of staff playing their daily bridge game.

After lunch, the chair was left untouched. The cleaners knew that they were expected to return the chair to its original starting place for the following day, when the whole ritualistic process started all over again.

I taught in D5, and the second member of the history team, taught in D4. This poor man had no discipline at all and even the good kids made fun of him. Strangely, he was impervious to their insults.

The first time I encountered him was when I found that there was a shortage of chalk in D5. Cursing silently to myself, I decided to venture next door to borrow some. I tapped on Mr B.'s door and made to go in. I found that it was locked. I peeped in through the glass panel, and witnessed a truly chaotic scene. The kids were playing hockey in the classroom! Mr B. seemed completely unperturbed by all this and was delivering a lesson on the Crimean War whilst sundry missiles and hockey balls whizzed past his head.

I banged on the panel and the kids immediately stopped their game and looked curiously towards the door. "Can I have some chalk?" I mouthed through the glass. He opened the door a smidgeon and poked his head around the tiny aperture.

"Why have you locked it?" I asked in amazement.

"Got to, little buggers will escape," he boomed, and repeated this remark three times over. I later discovered that he had a very curious habit of doing this. Meanwhile these kids really were trying to escape, one was already trying to squirm his way underneath Mr B.'s arm.

"Get back boy," he commanded. "If you had been at Sebastopol, you would have been cannon fodder." He then turned his attention to me. "You're fairly new aren't you? You won't last long here, love, they're all animals."

"F*** off you old w****r and let me out!" the squirmer bawled.

"Back! Back!" he bellowed, using his best lion tamer voice. "You see my dilemma, love. You'll have to seek chalk elsewhere."

"Yes," I said, incredulously. He re-locked the door and the hockey match resumed.

My friend Wally and I loved to talk to Mr B. because he was unintentionally funny. The pair of us found that we shared a free period with him on a Friday afternoon. Wally and I along with the R.E. teacher had formed the B. Appreciation Society. I must admit that sometimes we did laugh at him, but we were also genuinely fond of him.

Every Friday saw the same ritual.

"Mel, go and see if B. is coming to the staffroom."

I would then have to traipse over to D block to find him, or even walk up to the staff car park where he could be found repeatedly inspecting his precious car lest one of the 'cretins' as he sometimes called them, had scratched it. He performed the same ritual every day. He would park his car before registration in the morning

and then circle it three times, kicking the tyres as he did so. He was checking for punctures. At lunchtime, oblivious of the sixth form boys hanging out of their windows, bawling and laughing at him, he would return to the car and again circle it three times looking for damage. Having satisfied himself that it was safe, he would then pat his pride and joy and tell it that he would be back at four o'clock.

Search over, I would ask him if he wanted a cigarette with us in the staffroom. He was so mean that the three of us knew that he would sell his soul for a free fag.

"Will be with you shortly Madeline," he would boom. Every week I would remind him that my name was Melanie, only to be told, "Same thing, same thing, same thing."

Once we had ensnared him in the comfort of the staffroom, we would get him started on any topic that we could think of. We knew that whatever opinion we held on a given topic he would always opt for the opposite point of view.

I was reading a holiday magazine one afternoon when he decided to grace us with his presence. He never ever sat, preferring to parade restlessly around the room like some caged beast, fag in hand and pontificating on the chosen topic for the afternoon.

"Corfu looks nice Mr B."

"Have you been there Madeline? Don't bother. Dingy little people, in dingy little houses with dingy little streets. Take my advice and leave it severely alone."

He lived alone and had never married. He was in love with the games mistress who had joined the staff many years previously at the same time as him. He had asked her out years ago, but she had declined saying that she already had a boyfriend. She married the boyfriend and Mr B. never spoke to her again. She never gave up trying to speak to him though, but he stubbornly stared straight ahead whenever he met her in the corridor.

Eventually, the keen and energetic new headmaster who was going to re-invent the school, retired on the grounds of ill health, probably all down to chasing runaway kids through the woods. He had only managed two years.

A man who was dour, colourless and humourless replaced him. This one was sneaky and underhand. Mr B. became a thorn in his side and so he hatched and plotted until he forced him to take early retirement.

I would see him from time to time wandering aimlessly around the town.

"How's the school Madeline, you still dealing with the dross?" he would ask almost wistfully.

He was found dead on his kitchen floor only two years after his retirement. A heart attack. He had lain there for three days. He was only fifty-six.

The Geography Department

The geography department was also housed in D block. They were a funny lot. Sometimes when I went to teach over there they were great fun, and then on other occasions they could be morose and bad-tempered. The head of geography was also the deputy head. It was he who was responsible for the timetable and compiling a list of supply teachers if a member of staff was absent for any length of time. The kids and staff were petrified of him. He could fly into uncontrollable rages at the least little thing. Needless to say that he didn't have any discipline problems.

He was very keen on the ladies and would make a beeline for any new and pretty member of staff. There was one supply teacher whom he always used as a stand-in. She was slim, blonde and very pretty, but a useless disciplinarian. Staff spent all their time having to sort out problems in her classroom.

According to the children, the deputy had a filthy habit of picking his nose and surreptitiously depositing his snot underneath the teacher's chair. I didn't believe them and told them not to be so cheeky and personal about a member of staff.

"He does, Miss, we seen him," and they all nodded in unison.

On my next visit to D block I found that I had no class. This was due to the fact that the R.E.

master had kept them behind because they had been unruly in his lesson. I was alone in the deputy head's room. I kept thinking of what my class had said and decided that as there was nobody in the immediate vicinity, I would take a look. I turned the large teacher's chair upside down in order to get a better view, and sure enough there was the evidence!

"Ugh!" I yelled, and let go my grip on the heavy chair. The result was that the deputy who was enjoying a free period and a fag in his office next door, came to investigate the cause of the disturbance. I didn't see him coming as I was trying to right the cumbersome chair before my class arrived.

"Anything wrong, Miss Phillips?" I jumped backwards and screamed loudly.

"No, Mr J.," I lied. "I thought that I'd put my hand in chewing gum as I pulled the chair forwards to sit down, but as it turns out, there was nothing there."

I could sense that he knew I was lying, but he merely gave me a terrifying glare and disappeared. At this moment the kids came tumbling into the room.

"Have you had a look under his chair yet, Miss? There's heaps of it, all gone 'ard like cement!"

"Don't be ridiculous," I lied. "Get your exercise books out!"

Second in the department was a poor old boy who was very close to retirement. Why he had not chosen to leave before was a mystery to me. He was one of the few remaining teachers left over from the days when the school had been a grammar. Most of the other staff had fled as soon as the word 'comprehensive' had been uttered. They had snatched at the early retirement package and had opted for the stress-free life.

This poor old dodderer had taught me many years ago and even we used to play him up. He was so boring. All he did was dictate notes and walk around and around the room kicking at pencil shavings that we had deliberately scattered on the floor, knowing that he detested them.

All pretty mild stuff really. However, those days had gone. Some of these kids weren't just naughty they were evil and cruel. Consequently the poor old bugger had a terrible time of it. He had a very bad nervous twitch, which made him spasmodically jerk his head to the left. He had a habit of pacing quickly around the room and then stopping suddenly, to absentmindedly gaze out of the windows. These hooligans would deliberately leave the windows open so that he would inadvertently bang the side of his head on the glass.

However, he finally called it a day when he opened his large teacher's desk to get out some of his text books. Sitting in the middle of the pile of books was a package neatly wrapped in pink gift paper. It was addressed to Mr W. He unwrapped it eagerly. He recoiled in horror as the contents of the package were revealed. Some depraved yob had gift-wrapped a parcel of human crap!

The Insane Artists

Sometimes the deputy head would hand you a 'pink slip'. Everyone moaned when they received one of these because it meant that a member of staff was absent and you had to cover their class.

I always dreaded getting a pink slip, especially if it was to go down to the metalwork and woodwork departments, or worse, having to trail off to the woods to supervise the rural science lot. The teachers of these subjects deserved a medal because some of these beauties were violent and abusive. However, sometimes you would get a slip to go to the art suite, and I loved a chance to go up there.

There were three members in the department, two men and one lady. They were such a happy bunch. Their radio continually blasted out pop music. One of the men was a fantastic cartoonist and had drawn a cartoon of the old headmaster running through the woods in hot pursuit of some truant.

Pete was a potter and was head of the department. The children used to fall over themselves in the fight to get to his lessons. He was eccentric to the point of insanity and the kids delighted in his madcap antics.

I recall the time when Phil, the second in command, brought a bunch of daffodils into the art staffroom to use as an aid to a still life drawing. Pete whipped out one of the blooms and waited until Phil's class was underway.

"Take this flower into Mr J.," he whispered to a little girl, "and give it to him. Tell him that the message from Mr R. is, that he loves him with all his heart and he will give him a kiss at dinner time."

Pete was also an atheist and detested Thursdays. Thursday was the day when the vicars came to conduct morning assemblies. He would hide on these mornings complaining that, "A festering of vicars had taken over the school. There are bloody dog collars everywhere," he would grumble.

There was one vicar per year group. Ours was a great fat, wheezy old man. He was strict and stern like most Methodists are. I didn't like him because he refused to allow his poor son to go on school trips, considering them to be frivolous and of no worth.

My colleague and I had been admonished by him (quite rightly so) for laughing whilst he was delivering his sermon. She and I had been listening to his boring address as he reflected on the existence of angels.

"I have seen an angel," he told this bunch of shuffling, disinterested kids. At this point a boy sitting close to us said quite loudly to his mate, "He must have been on the f*****g heroin."

The pair of us burst into uncontrollable laughter and were later forced to apologise for our unseemly behaviour.

I begrudgingly explained to him that I was very sorry for my behaviour, but if he hadn't been so boring in the first place I should have been listening to him.

My head of year, although amused, advised me to keep out of his way and so it was that Pete and I ended up looking after the kids who didn't go into assemblies, such as Jehovah Witnesses, Catholics and sundry naughty delinquents who weren't allowed anywhere near a religious assembly.

I used to look forward to these mini interludes once a week, mainly because Pete made us all laugh.

However, he was soon to leave, having got himself a good job as an art lecturer at the local teacher training college.

The week before he left, we were in our usual Thursday room, when he told us all that he was leaving. Some of the pupils were very upset.

"You really should be glad for me children," he announced. "I am going to a place where I shall be able to wear my own striped underpants and in any colour I fancy."

"Don't tell lies, Sir," one of them laughed.

"It's true, don't you realise that Miss Phillips and I have to wear regulation navy blue school knickers with a pocket in the front? As from tomorrow I shall be a free man. Be delighted for me. As for our Thursday meetings, Miss Phillips will carry on the worthy cause of atheism. She will carry on the fight to rid the world of vicars! Bye bye and good luck."

They Were A Law Unto Themselves

Over on the other side of the building, tucked out of sight, and out on a limb was the science block. The head of science had taught me when I was a pupil and had also taught my brother. He was not very tall, but he had a powerful presence.

He had been in the R.A.F. and did not tolerate fools gladly. He had perfected his own punishment for the boys. He had them bend over and touch their toes, then swish their arses with a length of Bunsen burner tubing. My brother said he would rather have had the cane any day because this punishment made the ends of your toes curl up. The girls did not escape either. He would keep them in detention for an hour; he spaced out the naughty kids so they couldn't talk to one another, then made them sit in silence with absolutely nothing to do. That was punishment.

You were required to knock before you entered the science staffroom, and then you had to state your business and leave as quickly as possible. This was their domain. They had their own tea and coffee making facilities and refused to join the other staff in the main staffroom.

The new head had decided that all subsidiary staffrooms must cease to be, and all staff must congregate in E block staffroom for the morning briefing and the ensuing coffee breaks. Most staff had reluctantly given up their peaceful sanctuaries, but not the science department. They refused to conform and so the head took away their chairs. Undeterred they stood up to drink their tea. Finally he took away their urn and so they were eventually smoked out of their lair. However, they were determined that they would make him pay for what he had done to them.

Staff meetings were held in the lecture theatre. The science boys retaliated by barracking the head at every given opportunity. They were so rude. We loved to see them arrive at a staff meeting because you knew that a fracas of some kind would develop.

When school finished at the end of term we all loved a good session at the rugby club. However, this lot were hitting the booze at mid-morning break. They would be pissed by lunchtime.

I once walked alongside the head of science as he weaved his way to final assembly in the main hall. A young boy passed us going in the opposite direction.

"Where are you going boy?" he slurred.

"On a message for the secretary, Sir."

"Well f*****g well hurry up or you'll be late for assembly."

They don't make them like that anymore!

The Exclusive Club

One particular morning the humourless head called an emergency staff meeting. It appeared that a person or persons unknown had been crapping in various places around the school building. Dollops of it had been found on the main stairs, D block, and even on the changing room fioor. The head was very concerned about this matter and wanted our full cooperation in finding the culprit.

"Anybody who finds some human excrement, please report the matter to me immediately," he said.

It just so happened that a few days later I was teaching drama to a class of kids in the main hall. The children were performing on the stage.

"I can't hear you," I shouted. "I am going to stand at the back of the hall and I want your delivery to be loud and clear."

I walked to the back and as I did so I nearly trod in a gigantic turd.

'I had better report this immediately,' I thought.

I tapped on the head's door and waited for him to summon me inside. Whilst I waited, I could feel suppressed laughter welling up to the surface. Eventually, he opened the door.

"Yes, Miss Phillips?"

"I have found some excrement, Mr P." I stumbled.

He stared at me and without a fiicker of amusement on his face said, "Was it fresh?"

I burst out laughing and said, "I don't know. I'll go back shall I and take a bite out of it?"

"Don't be facetious with me, Miss," he glowered, "I am trying to establish a time. You can go now."

Of course I told the whole staff. Damn me if only a few days later the bloke who taught next door to me, and another member of our department, found some too.

John, made three badges which said, 'The I've been Shit On Club.' You couldn't join unless you had had previous experience.

They eventually found the kid who was doing it and he was expelled. I always thought that he must have had the most cooperative of bowels.

A New Experience

The head called a staff meeting early in 1987 and announced that the school needed to lose ten teachers as the number of children on roll had fallen drastically. If anybody felt that they needed a change of school and should like to be redeployed in a locality which suited them, he would arrange it.

My friend and I felt that we needed a change of scenery and very soon he had his ten volunteers. Nine of us were soon fixed up with new secondary schools, mostly in their local area, but because I couldn't drive I was proving more difficult to place.

Eventually the head called me into his office and said that he had found a good junior school for me.

"I'm not going to a junior school!" I retorted.

"Well there's a secondary twenty miles from here," he said.

"That's no good to me," I sulked.

"Try the local junior and see what you think."

In teaching there exists a very snobby three-tier system. Secondary teachers look down on junior staff and juniors look down on infants. Awful, but true. I was no different in my opinion.

"I'll go down and have a look, but I'm not taking it."

As I walked to the school, I was thinking about different ways in which I could successfully fail this interview.

When I arrived I was ushered into the staffroom and asked to wait for the head. I hadn't been waiting long when a bloke with permed hair similar to Kevin Keegan's, strode into the room.

"Cup of coffee?" he was very friendly.

"Yes please," I replied.

"Fag?"

"Thanks."

"Blessed art thou amongst women," he said, dramatically. "Nobody else smokes. They're always on my back. What have you come for?"

I told him.

"I hope you get it. I'll have an ally at last."

He drank his tea and left. I could see the head's room from where I was sitting.

Suddenly his door opened and this shifty, skinny kid almost fell out.

"I'll clash your backside if you do it again!"

"Sorry about that, Miss. Little bugger has just dismantled my new calculator. A member of staff sent him to me to be disciplined and that's what he did whilst he was waiting. You've come for the appointment. It is Mrs O.'s maternity leave, so we are talking about a year."

"What will I be expected to teach?" I said. I had had no experience of small kids.

"Why everything, Miss!"

Here was my opportunity. My opting out clause. "I can't teach maths," I said, truthfully. "I'm an English teacher."

"Oh you'll only be required to teach it to nine-year-olds."

"I had a C.S.E. grade nine in maths, I really can't manage it."

"I admire your honesty," he said, sitting back in his chair. In that case Mr R. can teach all the maths in year five and you can teach all the English."

Foiled.

He took me on a tour of the school, which was completely open plan. He explained that every year had an open area that was used for art or fioor space for assembly. Whilst he spoke I was mesmerised by a scruffy bloke who was screaming and bawling and throwing a kid around like a rag doll. I recognised him as the same weasel I had seen coming out of the head's office previously.

"Excuse me," I ventured. "Who is that?"

"Oh, that's Mr B. Take no notice, Miss, we all have our crosses to bear."

With that he left me in the capable hands of Mr R. and swept away.

"Welcome to the world of primary education," he laughed.

'Oh well, I can stick it for a bit,' I thought to myself. I ended up staying sixteen years.

Get On With It!

I soon realised that the transition from junior to secondary is relatively easy, but not the other way around. There was so much to learn that I really needed re-training, but needless to say I wasn't offered any by the local education authority.

I had come from a secondary school where all classes were set according to their needs and abilities. There was no setting system here, they were all mixed ability and I had no idea how to organise them. I was, quite simply, lost.

The first time I met my class of nine-year-olds, I shouted at one naughty boy and a number of the class burst out crying! I wrote very quickly on the board in cursive writing, and there was a general cry of, "We haven't done joined-up stuff yet!"

My printing was useless. I was required to make visual aids and to decorate the walls. The walls were also an issue. They had to be festooned with borders and lining paper. The kids' pencils, rulers and trays had to be labelled with their names on them. Charts showing the months of the year and the times tables had to be displayed around the room. One evening I spent a good hour with my tongue between my teeth, printing and copying out the days of the week as part of a wall display, only to find on finishing that I had missed out Thursday.

A kind member of staff showed me something called 'classroom organisation', whereby the children were put onto tables according to their ability. This resulted in four separate worksheets, all differentiated, but on the same topic.

Then there was the photocopying. In my previous school you simply handed in your photocopying a day in advance and then collected it from one of the four school secretaries. Here you had to do it yourself. I was used to handing in my register every term and not being too fussy if it balanced or not. It was impossible to do that here.

A sepulchral voice would come over the tannoy system every four weeks with the dreaded message: "May I remind you ladies and gentlemen, that it is the end of the month."

This meant that you had to make sure that your register balanced and then submit it to the head who was very fussy about legal documents. He had once worked in a bank. My maths was so bad that no matter how hard I tried, I could never get the thing to balance. The head knew that I was hopeless, but would keep me behind after school when everyone had gone home in order to find the mistake myself.

"You show me, Mr D." I would plead.

"No, Miss, you've got to learn by your mistakes."

Also there were physical problems to overcome. Previously, when a child was sick in class, the caretaker was summoned to clean it up. Not here, you had to set to and do it yourself.

Similarly the teacher was responsible for other

little accidents and you were also required to adopt the role of surrogate mother as well.

"Miss, can you tie my shoe laces?"

"Miss, can you open my orange," (this always made me laugh) or, "open my pop, lunchbox?" etc.

"Will you undo my mac, the zip's stuck?"

"My plait's come undone."

I found myself tending to scraped knees, pulling out wonky teeth, checking for nits. The list was endless. Listening to the endless tale bearing, and then of course there was the tapping. Oh, the tapping!

Regardless of where you were, or if you were talking to a member of staff, the head, anyone, they would tap your arm in the same place, or pull your jumper to gain your attention.

"Miss! Miss! Miss!"

"I'm talking."

"Miss!"

I would eventually turn around and tap them in the same spot on their arms or tug at their clothes. They would look at you in astonishment.

"What you doing, Miss?"

"Just wondering if you would like it if I did it to you."

My words fell on stony ground.

I repeated the same instructions over and over daily, and heard myself perpetually saying, "Wipe your snobby nose. Whose snobby hanky is this on the fioor? Don't swing on the chair. You bite that rubber in half again you won't get a new one. Who put these pencil shavings on the fioor?"

AHHHHHHHHHHHHHHHH!

The Staff

There were about twenty-six members of staff, sixteen of whom were teachers, and the rest were teaching assistants. I had been used to a teaching staff of one hundred and twenty!

Amongst the staff was a teacher called Gwyn. He was one of the most eccentric people I have ever met. He travelled to school every day from Cardiganshire, where he ran a lucrative little sideline business making coracles. He also earned a cut out of every coracle postcard sold to visitors, because it was his picture on the postcard carrying his coracle on his back. He also had a coveted salmon fishing licence and fished on the Teifi. He sold his catch to the local pub. All in all he was very rich and very mean (as most Cardis are).

He taught Welsh. When I say he taught, I mean that he turned up every day. He got away with doing the minimal amount of work. Nevertheless, the kids and the staff loved him. He had led the most incredible life.

At the age of twenty-one he decided to row his coracle all the way to France. He even made the national news. He actually made it into French waters, but the authorities turned him away and declared his coracle to be an alien craft.

A few years later, he and a few of his rugby mates decided that they would see in the New Year in London, notably Trafalgar Square. Gwyn decided to take the coracle with him. They travelled with it strapped onto the luggage rack. On arriving in London, he took the craft off the roof rack and strapped it to his back. Midnight came and our hero decided to jump into the fountain in Trafalgar Square and started to row around it in the coracle. The crowds applauded and everyone screamed with laughter. He then made a quick exit from the fountain, having extradited himself from the coracle and nimbly dashed into the crowd, whereupon he began to run on his hands. This was his party piece. He had been a gymnast before he had gone to seed. However, he was nabbed by an on-duty policeman, who locked him in a police cell for the night where he was charged with causing an affray and making a public nuisance of himself.

He always suffered with stomach problems and was continuously slugging indigestion mixture. He had an ulcer that was a direct result of too much booze. One morning he arrived at school, moaning about his stomach and blaming the laver bread he'd eaten the night before, for his plight. The deputy head said to him, "When you go home tonight, pour yourself a port and brandy. It settles your stomach in no time."

"Duw, Duw," he said, "I'll have a bash at that."

The next morning when I walked into the staffroom I could hear the sound of loud vomiting emulating from the men's toilet.

"Who's bad?" I said.

"Gwyn," said the deputy.

With that, an ashen and shaky Gwyn staggered

into the room, he was stinking of booze.

"What's the matter with you?" I said.

"Him. Him and his daft advice."

"What have I done?" said the deputy, in surprise.

"You told me that port and brandy was good for my guts."

"Yea."

"Well I had twenty-four and I feel bloody worse."

It was rumoured that his cottage in Cardigan was stuffed full of antiques. He had told us about his postcard collection, which was worth ten thousand quid alone.

I had never been to his place, but a mate of mine had and she said that instead of wallpaper, he had newspaper plastered onto the walls. On this particular day we were discussing his collection of half-hunter watches and how much we thought they were worth. All of a sudden one of the teaching assistants piped up, "I didn't know that Gwyn kept horses." You often wondered where they got the staff from.

However, matters became very difficult for Gwyn. A new Welsh advisor had been appointed to the county and she was very keen. It was her job to go around schools making sure that the Welsh language was being taught properly. She wanted to see a selection of Gwyn's work. What was he to do? He had no visual aids, no examples of children's work, he was sunk. He was so lazy that he had nothing to show this woman. His charm failed to work on her. She was a lesbian. She wanted examples of work and she wanted them very soon.

The head called a 'save Gwyn meeting' and we were all so soft and daft that we set to and made him some visual aids to give to the adviser.

"Well, bloody hell, I don't know what to say," he stuttered. Duw Duw."

After a while however, the butch adviser saw through him and us, and gave him an ultimatum. She couldn't sack him, but she could make his life a misery. She made regular checks to the school.

Suddenly Gwyn developed a very bad back. He was in excruciating pain. All that driving from Cardigan and back every day had given him a crooked spine and, coupled with his peptic ulcer, he really was in a bad way. He would have to take early retirement on health grounds.

We had a big party for him and gave him a good send off. To celebrate his success he did his party piece and ran around the room on his hands. Sly devil!

A One-Off Job

I have seen some strange and queer staff in my teaching career, but none to compare with Mr B. The odd thing was that those who had taught in the school with him for a long period of time simply accepted the way he behaved, but for a newcomer to the staff like me, it was mind-boggling.

The man was quite simply mad. Firstly, there was his appearance. He wore terrible clothes. His jackets were too short in the arms for him and his trousers, that flapped at half mast, were kept in place by a pair of huge braces. He wore sandals with socks. His hair stuck straight up on end and he had a habit of absentmindedly scratching the top of his head. He was also rather smelly.

He managed to get himself into some amazing scrapes. He came to school one day and the head took one look at him and told him to go home and change his clothes. He was actually wearing two ties and had his underpants on outside his trousers!

He was an even worse teacher than Mr B. from the comprehensive school. He taught next door to me and as the classrooms had no roofs (all open plan) the noise which filtered through from his room to mine was deafening.

He shook the kids until their teeth rattled, and all the while he bawled and screamed at them to be silent, but to no avail. His own teeth were permanently clenched. His face purple with suppressed rage. He loped around the room snarling and spitting insults, whilst they just laughed at him.

He had strange habits. He would stay behind after school until about half past five at night, waiting for his fierce wife to pick him up, and then, when everyone had gone home, he would raid their rooms for classroom equipment. He didn't have any equipment himself because the kids had pinched it all, not because they wanted it, but because they could.

I was working late one night when I saw him stealthily enter my room; he didn't see me tucked away in the corner. I watched fascinated, as he rummaged through my drawers, filling his pockets with marbles. We used the marbles for maths. They were used to weigh different objects. My marbles had been slowly disappearing from my jar and I had been blaming the kids. I waited until his pockets were full and he was about to go, then I shouted at the top of my voice, "Can I help you Mr B.?" He nearly leapt out of his skin. "What are you doing in my room?"

"I was just checking your marbles, Miss. I suspect that my class have been secreting them into your jar."

"Yea," was all I could manage to say.

There was a huge notice on the photocopier in the staffroom that read, "Mr B. Do not touch this machine."

When I inquired why this was, I was told that he had broken three already!

He came to school one morning and the deputy head said to him, "Have you lost something, Sir?"

With that he jumped out of his seat and ran out of school. It materialised that he had driven to school and parked the car in the middle of a very busy road whilst he got out to post a letter. He then walked to school, leaving the car, still in the middle of the road with the engine running.

He retired shortly after I arrived. My friend Liz and I were sorry to see him go. He brightened up our day. You never really knew what he was going to do next.

The Whirlwind

The lady teacher, who taught year four, was the most energetic woman I have ever seen. She wasn't young, but she had the get up and go of a twenty-year-old.

Mrs D. lived about three miles out of town and in the summer she would leave her car at home and walk to school, wearing the highest of stiletto heels.

She was very clever at sewing and embroidery and made all her own clothes, including her handbags. She was also very religious and would spend her sewing lessons with the kids, stitching great long tapestries, all with biblical themes. The hall was bedecked with the Ten Commandments, the Lord's Prayer and many more, all lovingly worked by her and her class.

She never took a tea break. She didn't eat or drink all day. She was painfully thin, but still possessed this abundance of energy. Mrs D. could often be seen perched on precarious, rickety and makeshift apparatus that she utilised in order to mount her wall displays. The headmaster was always telling her to get down from her unsteady perch and leave the work to the caretaker, but she wouldn't listen.

Weekends saw her climbing the sea cliffs, still in high heels, in search of rock samphire, that awful, salty succulent, otherwise known as sea asparagus, which grows out of rocks. Apparently it's very good for you. It was widely used in Tudor times, but then they didn't have much else in the way of vegetables. She literally lived on it. She made soups out of it and even put it in her tea.

She was adamant that she suffered from narcolepsy, a condition that puts you to sleep in an instant as soon as you relax. This was unfortunate, because as soon as she sat in her teacher's chair and relaxed, or attended a staff meeting, she would instantly fall asleep, sometimes hitting her head on the blackboard as she did so. Personally, I don't think she had the condition at all. She was just exhausted from rushing around all day without any food.

She was never absent from school, even turning up for work with hacking coughs and snotty colds that she generously shared with everyone. However, she unexpectedly caught a condition called farmer's lung. Which I always thought was rather strange, as it is a condition associated with mouldy hay or corn! The condition unfortunately affected her so greatly at the time that she was forced to take ill health retirement.

I still see her. She must have got over her illness, as she is still racing about. I often wonder if she's still eating that bloody samphire!

A Bit Cramped

I had been teaching in the junior school for around two years when the education authorities decided to close one of our local infant's school and amalgamate them with us. Obviously the infant staff had been very happy where they were and were resentful of the move. However, after they had settled themselves in (which was a feat in itself considering all the gear they brought with them!) they settled down fairly well.

Their department was joined to our school, but yet it had its own classrooms within the building.

One of my friends taught in the infant department and kept me abreast of some of the funny episodes that occurred from time to time. For example, the little ones had an on-going project that involved dinosaurs. This particular day my friend told me that there was a terrible smell in her classroom. She sniffed and poked into every nook and cranny, but couldn't trace the source of the pong.

Weeks went by, until one little girl happened to say, "Mrs D. this dinosaur doesn't smell very nice." When she went to investigate, she found the source of the niff. Some kid had crapped himself, or perhaps herself, and had managed somehow to stuff the shit up the dinosaur's plastic orifice, which was located under its tail. My friend often used to ponder over three questions:

"Where was I? Why didn't I see it happening?" and thirdly, "Who did it?"

She never found out.

On another occasion, the children came in after their playtime and some of them were heard to remark very loudly, "Dennis has had an accident, Miss, he's trod in dog's muck."

Further investigation revealed that Dennis had not trodden in dog muck; he had actually crapped himself, to the extent that he had even filled up his shoes.

Mrs D. immediately took him to the boys' toilets where she discovered the extent of the mess. In short, Dennis was plastered from head to toe in shit. He was stripped off and was told to stand in an old Belfast sink whilst Mrs D. went in search of the necessary accoutrements required to clean him up. However, Dennis proved to be too slippery to get a purchase on, so much so, that he fell out of the sink and landed on the tiled fioor onto his head. Luckily he was so rough and tough that he bounced. He sat on the fioor for a while and then shook himself. He was scrubbed and dressed in clean clothes. The infants always kept a plentiful supply of clothes out of necessity. His soiled garments were wrapped in three plastic bags and handed over to his mother.

I would do anything to be invited to the infant nativity play. It was the major event of their year. The kids had to be kitted out, towels had to be purloined, wings and haloes had to be made and parents' airing cupboards raided. There was always the risk of some child being ill at the last minute or falling down and hurting itself, so all in all it was a very stressful day. I remember a member of the infant staff arriving for break in the staffroom just before the commencement of the play. She was close to tears as she dragged deeply on her fag.

"I don't know what I'm going to do," she wailed. "One of the wise men has fallen down and hurt his leg and the lamb's got measles, which means that I've got to f*****g baa all afternoon instead!"

Finally there was Paul. Paul suffered from Tourette's syndrome and was prone to shouting out swear words at inappropriate times. Obviously he was a special needs child, but he was also very intelligent.

Morning school assemblies were very dull and boring, but not on the occasions when Paul was allowed to attend. Staff and kids alike used to nudge one another expectantly and the whisper would go around the hall, "Paul's in."

He never disappointed. You could usually time him. He hated the Lord's Prayer. I don't know why, perhaps it was the unexpected silence, however, he would take the opportunity to shout f*** you or f*** all of you, before his carer dragged him through the door.

His mum used to collect him every day from school and would be waiting outside the classroom for him. He was making a Mother's Day card this one afternoon and had drawn a crude drawing of a person. He had then scribbled furiously over the whole thing because he had been told off that afternoon for swearing. He was still scribbling furiously when my friend said to him, "Lovely picture of Mummy, Paul." No reply. "Has Mummy got a fur coat on?" she was referring to the scribble all over the drawing.

"No! No!" he retorted. "It's her big fanny, big fanny!" At this point the staff looked up to see his mum waving and smiling at him through the door.

Authentic Lessons

And then there was me. My science lessons had to be authentic. Our project in year four was the human body. I decided that what I needed was a skeleton. I was a member of the Red Cross at this time and decided to ask them if I could borrow their skeleton. The instructor was very kind and allowed me to borrow it, but told me to be very careful with it as it was very old and very delicate. It came packed in a coffin-like wooden box and was delivered to my mother's house.

"What ya got in there?" she asked, trying to peep inside the lid. I removed it and brandished one of its femurs at her.

"Look at him, he's very old, Vera said I could borrow him."

"That's enough, Melanie," she shouted, in a panicky voice, put that old anthraxy thing back in the box!"

"Don't you like him?" I said. By this time she was retreating from the room. I chased her up the stairs with it and poked the long bone up her skirt.

"Put it away, you Burke and Hare b***!" she screamed at me.

I sat on the stairs helpless with laughter and unable to defend myself as she belaboured me about the head.

I took the skeleton to school, complete with coffin. I laid out a purple cloth for a display and gently placed the bones on it. At this point my N.N.E.B. came into the room. She saw it and screamed very loudly, "There is no way I'm going to sit anywhere near that thing!"

Later that morning, the head came into my room. He had been informed of the new arrival.

"That's rather excessive isn't it, Melanie?" he grimaced and winced as he pointed in the general direction of the skeleton.

"No." I replied. "They ought to know about these things; anyway they think it's wonderful. They asked me why he wasn't in the ground and when I explained that he had donated his body for scientific research they were very happy."

So enthralled were they that I had to put a notice on the skeleton which said in big letters, "DON'T TOUCH". Big mistake. Say that to children and that's the first thing that they'll do. I came in from break one day to find one of them throwing the skull around (he was falling to bits).

A few days after his arrival I heard several of my class talking to two children from the class next door.

The kid from next door was boasting that they had a plastic torso in their room that had detachable organs which could be slotted back together, a bit like a jigsaw.

"That's nothing," one of mine was saying, "you want to come into our room, we got 'alf an 'ead!"

I needed one or two other accoutrements before I was ready. I had not long been to the dentist for my six-monthly check-up and whilst I was there I had asked the dentist what he did with the teeth he extracted.

"I throw them away," was his reply.

"Next time you have a good haul from someone's mouth, can I have them?" I said.

"I'll see what I can do," he replied.

I was walking down Pembroke main street one Sunday morning when a car drew up along side of me. It was the dentist.

"Do you still want those teeth, Mel?" he queried.

"Oh, yes please!"

"Here you are then." He plonked twenty teeth in the middle of my hand.

I took them home and stuck them in bleach. I then brought them to school where I again upset the squeamish and the weak-gutted. I deposited them in a Pringle pot; I then rattled the contents so that they clattered together like castanets.

I still needed more visual aids. I wanted a set of false teeth, or a false bridge, a plate would do. I had a set of wind up joke teeth, they were alright, but I wanted the real McCoy. Mam had a plate. It had three teeth on it. She didn't use it. There was a reason for this. She had been measured for the plate and when it arrived it turned out to be someone else's teeth! It didn't fit. The teeth were useless and the dentist refused to change them. She had still kept the plate and I knew where it was.

"Can I take your plate to school, Mam?" I asked.

"Yea," she said. She was only half listening.

The kids were intrigued.

"That's what will happen to you if you don't look after your teeth," I told them. I had the trick set reposing in a glass of water.

There were sounds of 'Ugh', as they were passed around the room.

"Are these your mum's, Miss?"

"Yes," I replied. They were fascinated. "What's she wearing now then?"

"Nothing," I replied.

"Just holes?"

"She's got others."

"Oh."

My mother used to come to school every Thursday to hear the children read and to generally help out.

"We saw your teeth, Mrs Phillips," they said. "You should have looked after them. Miss says that the sound of false teeth being dropped into a glass is the saddest sound in the world."

"Does she now?" She was raving mad.

"Look at this. They proudly showed her a fang that I had suspended in Coke to show them the dangers of hidden sugar. Did you drink a lot of this when you were little, Mrs Phillips?"

"I'll see you later," mother spit through clenched teeth.

That evening she was immediately on the attack. She was still mad, which made me laugh even more.

"You showed all those kids my plate. You even passed it round. I was mortified."

"You said I could take it."

"I know, but I didn't know you were going to tell them it was mine."

There is a sequel to this incident. On Monday 5th August 2008, I took possession of a new washing machine, my old one having finally died on me.

The men who brought the machine pulled the old one out so that they could replace it with the nice new shiny one. Suddenly, the young lad who was with them let out a very low groan. I followed his eyes and saw that he was transfixed with horror as he stared in disbelief at something that was lurking behind the old machine. His boss bent down and held aloft a stinking rotten yellow molar.

"Yours, love?" he said, with the utmost disgust.

"It's not mine," I started to splutter.

"Forget it; we've seen all sorts of nasties behind machines."

My turn to be mortified.

My Scrapes

I was always at the centre of any wrongdoing, and always the first to get caught out.

In the 90's the government decreed that there should be no smoking in the workplace. I smoked back then. I agreed with the ban, but it didn't help me with my dilemma when I wanted a fag. The school had an old building across the playground that has since been knocked down. My friend and I would sneak over there to have a crafty fag when school had finished for the day. The building was used occasionally for P.E. and also by a male peripatetic teacher who taught the violin. The corridor was long and you were able to see if someone was coming.

My friend and I were there this particular night and from our vantage point we could see Mr C., the visiting master, however he failed to see us and accidentally locked us in!

Almost immediately my friend became hysterical.

"We'll have to stay the night and I'm bloody petrified of spiders!"

"Calm down," I told her, "The after school club children are still here, we'll see if we can call to one of them through this broken window."

We waited patiently until eventually a kid playing netball flashed into view.

I bent down so that my face was almost pressed against the crack in the window and whispered, "Claire, Claire." The child was looking everywhere but my way. Eventually she spied me and shouted, "Miss, what you doing in there?"

"Mrs R. and I are trapped in here. Someone accidentally locked us in. Go and get Mr G. (deputy head, who was also a smoker and would therefore be sympathetic to our predicament) he's got the key. Don't get the headmaster, understand?"

Off she went, very excited to be party to this important mission.

After what seemed a lifetime we heard voices outside the building.

"She's gone and got the head," my friend whispered, in an agitated voice. "What are we going to do? We can't let on that we've been smoking. Let's tell him that we're having a clandestine lesbian affair."

"Let's not!" I replied, in a horrified voice. We stood and awaited our fate.

The door opened and there he stood.

"Well ladies and what have we here? You're both very lucky. If I hadn't had to stay behind for a governor's meeting I should have been on my way home by now. You must think I'm daft. I knew all along that you used this place for a sly drag. Well you might as well carry on now."

The outcome was that he allowed all of us smokers to carry on with our nefarious practices. The others were delighted and were glad of a legitimate place to smoke. We had done them a favour.

My second smoking escapade came very much later. Our school had closed, but a new state of the art school had been built for us across the road.

The school itself was magnificent, but we all missed the old one with its leaky windows and patched fiat roof. There was no chance of any crafty fag here, unless you crept into a wooden structure resembling a cage, but with no roof. This was where the rubbish was dumped waiting collection. It was a blind spot for the C.C.T.V. cameras and so therefore out of the way of the head. We must have been pretty desperate for a fag in those days because we stood inside that cage which was minus a roof in all weathers. It had a bolt on the outside of it. This bolt dropped down into a hole which was also on the outside thereby locking it.

I had named this cage the 'Wicker Man' after the creepy cult film staring Edward Woodward, the one where he gets burnt to death in a wooden cage.

I was late on parade one lunchtime and found myself alone in the cage. There was usually quite a gang of us gathered in there. It had to be a quick fag because we were expecting Japanese V.I.P.s at half past one and everyone was expected to be within their classrooms. I shut the door of the cage and to my horror the bolt dropped down into its hole on the outside thereby trapping me on the inside. I tried to poke my fingers out of the bars to lift the bolt, but my hands were too big and my fingers too fat to go through the spars.

"What the hell am I going to do?" I said, aloud. It was twenty past one, I had to be with my class at one thirty. I shouted for help and hollered and bawled, but all to no avail. Then I remembered my mobile phone. Thank God. I rang the school secretary.

"I only saw you a minute ago," she said.

"I'm trapped inside the Wicker Man," I tried to whisper.

"I'll come and fetch you."

She turned up and duly burst out laughing.

"You won't tell him, will you?" I demanded to know.

"'Course not," she promised.

Liar. Next week as we were all seated in the tedious weekly staff meeting the head asked for our full attention.

"If some of you want to kill yourselves by smoking, can you please make sure that you leave the door of the so called 'Wicker Man' open, so that there will be no need for a rescue operation."

Everyone turned towards me and burst out laughing including the head.

"It could only happen to you, Mel," he said.

Then of course there was the classic saga of the swan's neck.

From time to time children were sent to other classes for some misdemeanour or other. This was quite a common practice amongst the staff. This particular day I was in the middle of a history lesson with year three when the door opened and this sulky, truculent boy was standing there.

"What do you want boy?" I asked of him.

"Mrs L. has sent me, Miss."

"Why?"

"She said I give cheek to her, Miss, but I never."

"Sit down over there," I said, wearily, "And be quiet."

Year three was studying the Victorians and the lesson I was teaching just happened to be Thomas Crapper's waste water preventor. The children were roaring with laughter at the mention of his name and I was making them laugh with sundry lavatorial stories.

I noticed that the miscreant from year four was laughing fit to bust.

"We never have nothing funny in our history lessons," he said.

"Your class is studying the Tudors aren't they?"

"Yea."

"The Tudors were great," I said. "There are lots of funny stories about Henry VIII."

"What?" he sulked.

"Well, for a start Henry had a toilet with a black velvet seat and he had a servant called 'the groom of the stool' to wipe his bum."

Everyone was laughing by this time, including the naughty boy.

"And," I added, warming to my subject, "he had his bum wiped with a swan's neck."

There were screams of merriment. The bell sounded, indicating the end of the afternoon's lessons, and that was that.

The next day the head came into the staffroom after having done playground duty. He asked to see me.

"I have just had Ronald Davies come up to me in the playground asking me if it is true that Henry VIII wiped his backside with a swan's neck. Did you tell him that?" He was very serious.

"Of course I told him," I said. "How did you know it was me?"

"Who else?" he sighed.

"You ought to have known all about that," I said. "You've got a degree in history."

"They didn't teach us that in university. Oh, before you go, was it alive?"

"What?"

"The swan."

He was serious.

The School Inspection

In 1997 we received the dreaded 'brown envelope' that signalled an impending school inspection. The woman who taught next door to me immediately went into a blind panic at the thought of it, even though it was a year away.

We had endless meetings in preparation for the thing, and policies and documents for every subject. Sometimes we didn't leave school until nine o'clock at night.

I was determined as the months went by that I was not going to catch their anxiety, but of course some of their angst did rub off on me. I once sat bolt upright in bed and shouted, "I haven't got enough chairs in the hall for speaking and listening!"

We learned that the seven-strong inspection team hailed from Wrexham.

"I went to college there," I told my friend.

As the dreaded day came closer, the head sought me out and announced that the chief inspector, a Mr Belcher and head of the team, used to lecture at Cartrefle College, and had remarked on his pre-school visit that he was delighted to learn that an ex-'Cart' girl was on the staff. He had lectured in Cartrefle in the 60's.

I stared in horror. Oh no, it couldn't be the same bloke, but surely there couldn't be two Mr Belchers who hailed from Wrexham and had taught in Cartrefle College?

"What's his specialised subject?" I asked the head with some trepidation.

"Maths, but of course he will drop in on any subject you happen to be teaching at the time. Why?" he asked.

"He attempted to teach me maths once."

"And?"

"I was useless."

"Nothing changes," he said, rather unkindly.

"I also broke his Banda machine."

In 1969 the Banda had just arrived in schools. The college had purchased one at great expense. The students were required to familiarise themselves with this machine because we would need it to make work sheets for teaching practice. We all had a turn with it and I don't know quite what I did wrong, but all I know is that I buggered up the insides of it.

"Where are you from girl?" What did that have to do with anything.

"Pembroke."

"Get out of my sight." He was livid. I prayed he wouldn't remember me.

"It had to be you," the head tutted. "Why am I not surprised?"

There would be a whole week of being gaped at, questioned and investigated. There would be scrutinising of work sheets and the interrogation of children in order to see how much they had progressed or regressed. They would be sitting in the back of our classes, feverishly making notes.

The day finally arrived.

"I'm nervous, Mam," I admitted.

"Why," she said, "he can't give you a baby."

Every time I thought about that I laughed, but it didn't stop me wanting to pee myself with fright as I passed through the school gates on that Monday morning.

Nobody was given a timetable of their visits, although some staff grumbled that it wasn't fair. I thought that it was perfectly fair; it wouldn't have been a spot check if you knew when they were coming.

Monday came and went, but no visit for me. Some staff was regaling us with horrendous comments that had been passed about their work sheets and their delivery of their lessons. They're bound to come to me tomorrow I mused.

Tuesday, nothing. On Wednesday morning I had a visit. It was for a religious education lesson. I was pretty confident on this one because that had been my chosen subject in college.

The inspector was very pleasant and after the lesson had finished he asked me a few questions.

"By the way," he said, "I have been reading your C.V. You taught in Oswestry."

"That's right," I said.

"I attended that school as a pupil."

I groaned quietly to myself. I was surrounded by them.

"Did you know Mr W.? He taught me chemistry."

"Yes," I replied.

"Well," he enthused, "I shall have to come and see you again and we can renew our conversation."

"That'll be lovely," I lied.

The geography inspector came next, followed by the English specialist. 'Not too bad,' I thought.

Friday afternoon came. This was when the team were supposed to be leaving. We had been told that they would probably be no more visits, because they had to make their inspection report.

I taught art on Friday afternoons. We were discussing Edvard Munch's 'The Scream' would you believe? (for nine-year-olds!) and then we were going to draw and paint a picture of 'The Scream'. These poor kids were not only expected to absorb this difficult concept, but they were also expected to remember what they had learned about Monet, the previous year when they were only eight–year-olds.

They were also required to dress themselves appropriately from a central table that contained pinnies and shirts. They were supposed to pour the water into jam jars for painting by themselves and also give out the brushes and paints. The tables were already covered in plastic cloths.

I was in full fiow, telling them all about the strange life of Munch when the door opened and in came Mr Belcher.

"I couldn't leave before I had seen you," he enthused. "A student from Cartrefie. A rare species indeed!"

"Come in please," I managed to say, all the while thinking, 'You b*******, fancy dropping in at this late stage in the game.'

"The children are just about to gather up the necessary equipments required for the lesson." I babbled on.

Inspectors have an uncanny knack of picking on the thickest kid in the class to answer their questions.

"Who painted this picture do you think?" he asked poor old Stan, who was as dull as a brush, but very streetwise and comical.

"Edvard Much."

I was impressed.

"Can you remember anything about Mr Monet? You did drawings and paintings about his work last year, didn't you? Do you remember the names of any of his pictures?" He was pushing his luck now. To my relief and total amazement he said, "Yeah, he painted them water lilies," and then added, "And I dressed myself. Look."

He lifted up his pinny and underneath was another pinny!

"Good boy," he laughed.

'Too good to be true,' I thought. I was right.

"Give the water out would you Marcus." I smiled sweetly.

"OK."

With that he took the big metal jug of water and turning around to face me said, "Shall I pour some in the jam jars?"

"Yes."

I turned back to face the inspector and before I could open my mouth I heard this desperate scream.

He had accidentally poured the contents of the jug all over the art paper, all over the table and then drowned a little girl who was sitting in the corner minding her own business.

"Sorry, Miss."

My art lesson was ruined. There was water everywhere. I couldn't help myself. I burst out laughing.

"Well, it's literally back to the drawing board," I shrugged at him.

To my amazement he burst out laughing too.

"You kept your head," he said. "I am so used to perfect lessons in my job that it's refreshing to see everyday accidents and mishaps. That's what teaching is all about. None of us are perfect."

We had the report on Monday morning.

"Well, Mel," the head announced. "Mr Belcher told me to tell you that he loved your lesson. It was not the best art lesson he'd ever seen, but it was the funniest."

Best of all, he didn't remember that I had broken his Banda!

The Things Kids And Their Parents Say

Over the years my friends and I have acquired some lovely notes and howlers. Here are a few of them from the good old days when teachers had time to have a good laugh between themselves and there was no national curriculum.

Here is a note that was sent to me when I was teaching in my secondary school in the Midlands:

> Dear Missus,
> Shelmondine's not in school today because she has the diarria.

The word 'diarria' had been crossed out, as the mother, knowing that she had misspelt the word, tried once more. Her second attempt wasn't much better as she wrote diyerea. Finally, after crossing out the two incorrectly spelt words, she had given up and had written 'the shits'.

From my third secondary school, the games master had a note that read:

> Please excuse Julie from games today as she's hurt her hind legs.

And from my friend's primary school:

Dear Mrs Ford,
Brendan has a boil on his bum. I have sent him with some cream. You're his favourite teacher please could you put it in for him?

A retired ex-head from our primary school had a note given to him that read:

Sorry Brian wasn't in school yesterday, but he had diarrhoea through a hole in his shoe.

And finally what the kids say.

I always seemed to get the best howlers from my class because they would tell me everything, and I mean everything.

After I had marked the register in the morning I used to ask the class if they had any interesting news. On this particular occasion, we had just returned from a half-term holiday so they had plenty of news to tell.

"Miss, Miss!" One of my little girls said. "I went to Blackpool and we went up the Blackpool Tower in a big lift. My Mam don't like heights and she pissed herself."

"Miss, we went to a posh restaurant and my dad farted and everyone turned round and looked at him, and my Mum said, 'stop f******g showing me up, Paul.'"

164

A little boy came to me at playtime one day and whispered, "Miss, Vicky is swearing. She's using the R word again."

I wracked my brain for ages whilst I tried to think of a swear word beginning with R, but eventually I gave up. However, curiosity got the better of me and I said, "What did she say, Craig?"

"I can't tell you, Miss, it's too rude."

"Go on, whisper."

He looked around to see if anyone was listening and into my ear he whispered the word, 'ARSE'.

I took my class on a visit to the military cemetery one year. It was around Armistice Day and I was explaining about those men who had lost their lives in the two World Wars. As I was bending down over one grave and showing them the poignant inscription on the tomb, I felt little fingers parting the hair on the back of my head.

Suddenly the little girl got up and shouted, "You're a liar, Miss." She was really angry.

"What have I done?" I said.

"You said you had eyes in the back of your head and you haven't!"

The last remark came from a young girl who said to me during a speaking and listening lesson, "My dad's gone to France, Miss, he's coming back tomorrow."

"That's nice," I said.

"He's very kind, Miss, he's bringing back cigarettes and wine for all the men at the pub."

Well all that remains to say is that I retired in 2002 after thirty-two years teaching. I had taught sixteen years in secondary education and sixteen in primary, and enjoyed them equally. They were both great experiences and made for a very long and colourful career.

I was given a marvellous party and some wonderful gifts. However, the best compliment was given to me by the lady who used to collect our dinner money every morning.

When she used to arrive at our classroom door she would always say, "I can hear you lot laughing all the way down the corridor."

She sent me a retirement card and on it was written, 'The sparkle has gone out of year three.'

I thought that was the best compliment I'd ever had. It made you think that perhaps you weren't just another brick in the wall after all.